WEAR THE PEARLS

AND OTHER BITS OF WISDOM

CHRISTINE ASHWORTH

Copyright © 2019 by Christine Ashworth
All Rights Reserved.
ISBN No. 978-1-951663-00-1

No part of this publication may be reproduced, distributed, or transmitted, in any form or by any means, including photocopying, recording, or other electronic or mechanical methods, without prior written permission of the publisher, except in the case of brief quotations embodied in critical reviews and certain other noncommercial uses permitted by copyright law.

Foreword by Sylvie Fox
Edited by Sara Lunsford
Cover © by Scott Carpenter

Published in the United States by Christine Ashworth

http://Christine-Ashworth.com

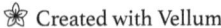 Created with Vellum

ACKNOWLEDGMENTS

There are a few people who, over the years, have suggested I put my Facebook posts into a book such as this one. Sylvie Fox, Diane Bentley, Greg Cunningham, this book is for you, with lots of love. I hope it meets your expectations.

None of this would have happened without the love and foresight of the amazing Alexis Morgan-Roark. Lady, I love you. You make me a better person.

Sara Lunsford, your guidance and love has been my saving grace. Bless you for believing in this book. Lots of love.

To everyone who has ever commented on one of my Facebook posts, shared it, or otherwise felt 'seen' as the saying goes, thank you so much for letting me know. This book is for you.

> The quality of mercy is not strain'd,
> It droppeth as the gentle rain from heaven
> Upon the place beneath. It is twice blest:
> It blesseth him that gives and him that takes.
> *--Portia, Merchant of Venice, Shakespeare*

FOREWORD

One morning I was scrolling through Facebook. I watched my friends get angry about politics, others celebrate writing milestones, and still more post pictures of their kids when I happened upon a post by Christine Ashworth that caught my attention. I think of it as the 'wear the pearls' post. It really touched me. You'll read it here in a few pages, but for me it may as well have been titled *carpe diem* or 'seize the day' or even 'a few hundred words that will change your life forever.'

That single post altered the trajectory of my time on earth in some profound and not so profound ways. First, *I wear the pearls* now. I wear them every day. I am wearing them right now while writing this at my computer in the middle of Los Angeles on a hot autumn day.

Not only do I wear the pearls, I wear the 'fancy' jewelry. I use the special soap. I no longer have guest towels. Instead have beautiful towels I share with guests who come to my house. I started living for today and not some unpredictable future.

With a few choice words, Christine changed my life that

day. I stopped delaying gratification when that delay was profoundly unnecessary. Keeping the pearls in their velvet box or the Tiffany necklace in a silk pouch or the Cartier tank watch in a drawer was providing pleasure for no one.

While I was reading *Wear the Pearls* I tried to think back to when I met Christine. Honestly, it's amazingly hard to pinpoint. Fiction writers in Los Angeles tend to find each other through one group or another. For us it was likely the Los Angeles chapter of Romance Writers of America sometime in the last fifteen years. It's an organization with some wonderfully supportive members. I've met many of my best friends at these meetings.

While I love romance writers, and I am one, Christine is more than a romance writer, she's the author of this amazing little book in your hands right now. She has a profound sense of judgment and a lot of wisdom from a life well and truly lived and we're all lucky that she is sharing some of that with us in this volume.

Wear the Pearls is a book to keep by your bedside. I have one or two such books that I turn to when I need a silent pep talk, and this has joined their ranks. There's something for everyone here and I know that it will give you insight to living a deeper and more fulfilling life. Finding true happiness is never easy, but that doesn't mean we shouldn't try.

Sylvie Fox
Los Angeles, California
September 2019

1

WHY I WROTE THIS BOOK

I was looking at myself in the mirror one morning, as one does when getting ready to leave the house for an extended period of time, and a glint in my hair caught my eye.

I leaned forward. Peered into the mirror. Saw gray hairs scattered through my hair. Not thickly placed, no - you have to really look to see them.

Then I looked again. They weren't gray hairs. Those were silver strands, just shimmering there against my mousy brown hair.

Silver.

I haven't colored my hair in a long time - almost a year at this point - and to see those silver strands made me smile.

I'm ready for the last third of my life. Excited and a little bit wide-eyed as I make some much-needed changes in how I live day to day.

I'm writing this book to take a look at where I've been, and how I'm going to make this last third of my life the very best I can. I'm not willing to be a fragile old lady. I plan to be strong and healthy to the end of my life, however I end up leaving this world.

And what I mean by the last third of my life, well, I look at it this way. I was a maiden until I became a mother at thirty. Now, with sixty knocking on my door (February of 2020), my parenting years are (mostly) over, the children are grown and I'm ready to become the wise woman, the crone. She Who Loves. I'm fine with that nickname for the next thirty years.

You know how some days you are going along, driving the route you always drive to get to where you need to go, and then you miss a turn? And everything goes from bad to worse before it gets straightened out again?

Sometimes that's what happens in our lives. We miss, or turn down, an invitation, a job, a relationship, an opportunity, a chance to learn and grow. And because we missed that chance, our lives changed. Perhaps we went down a path that hadn't been a part of our plan. Instead of taking a few minutes to get back on the right path, sometimes it takes us years.

Do you feel like something's missing? Are you struggling to find your way back to the path you were on? Or are you just now realizing that the path you're on is winding down for you, and it's time for a different path? Are you keeping your eyes open for opportunity, or are you just slogging through life, your eyes on the sidewalk in front of you so you don't trip? (I get it, I do.)

I've been edging around this new path, and with this book I am stepping firmly onto it. I'm scared, not gonna lie. Luckily, I have hands holding mine. If you need a hand while you navigate your path, my hand is open to you. You are another reason I wrote this book.

Wherever you are in your journey, whatever path you

are contemplating, walk it with an open heart. Walk it with wonder and joy.

One More Thing...

I begin this book with describing some pretty serious medical stuff. Not for sympathy, not for the "ouch factor," but to illustrate how my life had a few detours that I hadn't expected, and in the long run they changed me. Changed everything. That's why the medical stuff is there. (Oh...and I swear some, here and there. Just saying.)

The dated Facebook posts I share here started as lectures to myself, or things I really wanted to say to FB at large (or specific people that maybe wouldn't listen to me directly) that I put up on my profile. Then I had people tell me I should put them into a book. Recently, another friend said this book was needed, and I was the only one who could write it.

When I scoured my feed for interesting posts, I found that I only started to get preachy with myself in late-2015 onward. That, my friends, is when I felt the hatred of the masses infiltrate social media.

Inside this book is what I consider to be my antidote to that hatred. These are my thoughts and bits of my life. From my heart to yours. I hope it resonates.

This book isn't meant to be read straight through. Pick it up, put it down. Grab it when you might need a cheerleader to get you through a rough patch. Read a page or two, then move on. Or, heck, read it straight through. How you choose to read it is perfect.

Blessings to you and yours, and love, always.

~ Christine

2

...AND THEN I TURNED FIFTY

Life in my forties was fun, mainly because I didn't give a fuck the way I did in my twenties and thirties. I had left the big privately held computer company I had worked with for fourteen years and moved to an internet startup for a couple years. The kids running the place were in their twenties and had way too much money. Plus, they had substance abuse issues, and looked down on anyone not male. Thus, it was not too much of a surprise to learn I had been laid off in 2001 while I was in London, on vacation with my husband.

Tom took the day job to keep the family going, and I stayed home, writing, for much of my forties. The kids were growing, I was writing novels but hadn't sold yet, we took awesome camping vacations at Sherwin Creek, up in Mammoth Lakes. I also worked retail for Coldwater Creek for a few years (first as part-time, then as an Assistant Manager). I thoroughly enjoyed the work for the most part, but it was also the hardest physical work of any job (other than dancing) that I've ever done. Then I got laid off. Again. Ouch.

Wear the Pearls

In late-2009, I tried working in property management and learned, after working the job for four months, that just because I *can* do something, even though I may be good at it, doesn't mean that I *should* do it. So with my husband's blessing, I quit, just after I turned fifty. By the way, that's when he said my warranty ran out.

After I ran into my former manager at the mall, she told me there would always be a place for me, so I went back to work for Coldwater Creek. I also took odd jobs here and there. It was during one of those odd jobs that my life took a sharp turn.

I was helping my dear friend Bob Toschak[1] at a music teacher's convention in Los Angeles in July of 2010. We were setting up the day before the convention. He had boxes and boxes of sheet music for just about any type of musical instrument you could want. We set up racks for the music, added the sheets, put out tubs of music books of all sorts and styles on tables provided to us. We worked hard and finally called it quits well into the night.

I drove home from the Marriott near LAX to Simi Valley. At that time of night, it was usually a little over an hour drive. I kept having tunnel vision, which was scary. It would come and go, come and go. I kept to the middle lanes and drove at a reasonable speed, which is not like me, and breathed a sigh of relief when I made it home safe, well past the time I usually would have been home.

I didn't really think anything of it until the next afternoon. I was working the convention, helping people find music, making the sale if Bob was busy, talking to people, laughing, having a good time in my Hawaiian shirt (something Bob is known for at these conventions, so all his helpers wore them too).

But then the heads. All the heads, bobbing up and down

across the huge vastness of the hotel ballroom. Nausea caused me, more than once, to bolt for the bathroom. I felt off-kilter. Same thing the next day.

Then life, well. It went back to normal. Nothing alarming. Nothing unusual. The hubby[2] and I took walks in the summer evenings back then. As gentlemen do, he always put me on the inside of the sidewalk instead of next to the street. Except I kept bumping into him when he was on my right side. Weird. Just...weird. Right? So I made a decision, after the umpty-millionth time I bumped into him, to go to the doctor. Something was off, but I didn't know what.

Mid-August 2010, Tom was sitting at the picnic table he'd built me when we first bought the house in 1995. I think he was painting; I don't remember. The sun had set but the sky was still soft and light. I sat next to him, and told him I didn't know what was wrong, but I thought something was. I had started adding up the pieces, you see. So the next day I made an appointment.

Dr. Richard Lander. Bless the man. I sat on the uncomfortable exam table and explained everything while he sat and listened to me.

Dr. Lander didn't laugh at me and dismiss my concerns. Maybe it was because I told him I used to be a dancer, but he listened to me. I know, I'm lucky. He could have dismissed my concerns. I was a fifty-year-old woman complaining about her balance. So many doctors might have just patted me on the head and sent me on my way. Instead, he had me stand up. He put his hands on either side of my upper arms, about three inches away, and told me to close my eyes.

After less than ten seconds with my eyes closed, he gripped my shoulders and I looked at him.

We sat, and he told me there could be many reasons for my instability. Because apparently, when I closed my eyes, my balance went to shit quite violently without me being aware of it – my balance was totally out of whack.

He said it could be vertigo, but I didn't have the nausea (outside of at the Marriott). He said it could be an ear infection, but my ears didn't look inflamed. He said it could be a tumor on my auditory nerve but that was rare, so it probably wasn't that. However, it was time he turned me over to an Ear Nose and Throat doctor.

I met with the ENT a couple days later. After a brief visit with him, he ordered an MRI and rushed it through insurance. When I got home that day, his office called me with an appointment time for the MRI two days later. This rush rush bothered me. After the MRI (I mentally sang rock & roll songs while the banging and pulsing went on), I returned to the doctor a couple days later. Confirmation; I had an acoustic neuroma.

He told me I needed hearing tests, and I was rushed through that, as well. When the technician giving me the tests opened the door afterward, all sympathetic, I was crying. My right ear? Almost no hearing. I knew it before she told me.

Luckily, the ENT I had seen (I don't remember his name...sigh) had interned at UCLA Hospital, and under the Chief of Neuro-Otology, Dr. Akira Ishiyama, so he gave me that referral. I had an appointment with him for mid-September. Dr. Ishiyama would give us options.

Before that appointment, I reached out to a friend of mine who was a neurological nurse up in Spokane (and another person I'd known for over thirty years), and she dealt with this kind of thing all the time. She advocated for Gamma Knife Radiation.

I did some research. Radiation would only kill the tumor; it wouldn't remove it. And should the tumor regrow, the detritus (the dead blob of tumor) would make surgery more difficult. While there was no guarantee it would regrow, I quailed at the thought of being absolutely still for the radiation. Silly, but true. And the headgear I'd have to wear totally scared me to death. (This is a big reason to not go onto the internet when you're diagnosed with something. Seriously. Stay off!)

I went to see Dr. Ishiyama with a lot of fear. I learned later that his rate was $1,200 an hour. We were lucky in that a $35 copay handled it, thanks to the hubby and his Screen Actors Guild insurance plan. Seriously, this whole thing could have bankrupted us without that insurance.

Dr. Ishiyama spent over two hours with us, drawing diagrams, explaining what was in my head, and what we could do about it. He went over my options: doing nothing, as the tumor was slow growing; doing the Gamma Knife Radiation (and confirmed the part about radiation killing, but not removing, the tumor, making any possible future surgery difficult); or having surgery as my three options.

He talked about how the tumor, which was about the size of a dime, sat on top of both the auditory nerve (nerve #8) and the facial nerve (#7) on the right side of my face, and there was a chance that surgery could affect the facial nerve. Which would mean the right side of my face could droop if that nerve was disturbed. Never able to smile completely again...that was one of the risks.

He also mentioned a 5% mortality rate, mostly due to unexpected complications. Which I mentally turned into a 95% survival rate, but that 5% bothered Tom.

All that said, I voted for surgery. Tom, bless him, said whatever I wanted, he wanted. All I wanted was that intruder out of my head. When we made that clear, Dr. Ishiyama then referred me to the only neurosurgeon he would work with, because he was a perfectionist and methodical and got the job done. In 2010, that doctor also just happened to be the Chief of the Neurology Department at UCLA Hospital.

Dr. Neil Martin. We set up an appointment with him in October; the earliest we could get was six weeks away.

To combat the insanity floating in my brain, with Tom's blessing I fled to Colorado and spent the week with my best friend, Tammy Baar[3], in Snowmass. While I was there, I traded emails with Heather Howland, at the time an acquiring editor with Crescent Moon Press, now defunct. Before I left Snowmass, I had an offer from her to publish the first two books in my Demon series, Demon Soul and Demon Hunt (soon to be republished in the fall of 2019 as Fractured Soul and Warrior Soul). Talk about having a complicated autumn. Having my publishing dream come true, and having a tumor in my head, really kind of messed me up.

The days dragged by. I wrote like a fiend to get book one complete. Finally, it was time to meet Dr. Martin.

When he walked into the room, he was Captain and Commander in scrubs and cowboy boots, with three acolytes scurrying behind him with clipboards and pens. (They were either students or Residents...not sure, and no one introduced us.) Definitely romance hero fodder, he was easily 6'5", lean, mid-forties is my guess. Attractive, and in total control of his environment.

Where Dr. Ishiyama took time with us, and was open and approachable, Dr. Martin was all business, bordering on cold. Though he didn't look it, my guess is he was tired. (It was at the end of the day – I think the only appointment we could get was at 5:30pm on a Thursday or we could wait another two months for something earlier. Not wanting to wait, we took that late appointment and battled rush hour traffic to get there on time.)

He spoke clearly, concisely, about what he would do. There would be nodes on my face, to monitor my facial nerve responses and make sure his work wasn't affecting that nerve. The camera he'd use inside my head, which would show him what he needed to see. Cutting through my skull to get to the tumor, and the recovery time for something like that (3 – 6 months – ha).

I remember him being deliberately vague about how long this type of surgery would take. When he was done, we might have asked questions and he probably answered them (it's all kind of foggy at this point), and then he introduced me to his scheduling nurse and said to pick a time, if surgery was my decision.

It was.

His nurse gave me the option of December 16th or some day in January. When I dithered, she snapped at me. Apparently, there were many patients who needed surgery, but I was an interesting case, so he gave me a bit of preference. I chose December 16, 2010 to have the surgery. Another two months to wait.

After eleven hours of surgery, waking up first screaming in pain (which I don't remember, but my husband does, vividly) and then waking up again a few hours later to find six IV cannulas in me (two on each side of both hands, one in my neck, and one in my left ankle), I spent two days in ICU, then two days in a regular room. I went home on

December 21, 2010 and spent days afterward finding tape residue on weird spots on my body. Seriously.

All ended up well. The tumor is gone (benign – 99% of acoustic neuromas are benign), and while it took me three years to really get back to normal, all is well now. Except no hearing in my right ear, as they had to go through my Eustachian tube to get to the tumor. Hey, at least it wasn't through my skull, yeah?

Because of the surgery though, if you are on my right side and talk to me and I don't respond, tap my shoulder to get my attention. Or as I like to say, talk to the ear with the bling (four earrings on my left ear...only two on my right).

If you want other insight into what I went through, go to my website (http://christine-ashworth.com). Check out the blog and enter in the search bar the term acoustic neuroma. There are a couple of posts that detail that day, and the recovery period three years later. Other details? Just ask me. I'll tell you.

THE SECOND THING that shifted my life was the hysterectomy I had in August of 2012. I'm putting my first blog post about it here, because I think it's important. My takeaway now? Don't neglect your health.

July 2012...I had an illuminating gynecology visit last week. I had to go, because I had originally gone to my GP for blood in my stool; he examined me and said he thought I had fibroids in my uterus. I had a CT scan, which confirmed a diagnosis of 'an enlarged myomatomous uterus.' My bowel, as well as all my other organs, were peachy fine, though squished. The GP set me up with a Gynecologist and a Gastro-intestine doc, just to be on the safe side.

So, after the Gastro doc said I was fine, I met this nice gynecologist doc, probably in her mid to late 30's. We talked for almost twenty, maybe thirty minutes. After she went through my symptoms (I'll spare you the details), I then complained that for the past three or four years, when I turn sideways, I am not thin. I've always – *always* been thin sideways, and not so much straight on.

But I'm not thin anymore when I turn sideways. I've gained weight, but it's out of proportion to how I've been eating. Even with The Menopause hovering on my personal horizon, there was no real reason for the weight gain.

Plus, my energy is low. I wake up a lot at night, I have to pee ALL THE TIME, and I get indigestion – something I never have had, with the exception of the two times I've been pregnant.

Pregnant. That's it. I feel – pregnant. But ugly-pregnant, not glowy-pregnant. I feel as though my bladder is being pressed on constantly. I often have a bit of difficulty breathing, and I'll get odd aches and pains in my abdomen.

Plus, my periods. (Okay, I'm not sparing you the details.) The first couple of days, it's like Niagara Falls. Every hour on the hour I need to change my extra-super-duper tampon. At night I have to wear a huge overnight pad along with my extra-super-duper tampon. And even then, there are mornings where I'll wake up and find I've bled all over the sheets. Yeah – that makes a woman feel sexy.

My doctor was fabulous. Prior to the physical exam, she told me there are options – drug-wise, I can go on a drug that is fairly new here in the States and kind of expensive, but I would take it just for the two or three really heavy days of my period, 3 times a day, to cut the blood flow in half.

Or, I could go on the Pill, which would also lessen the blood flow, but with hormones involved, I'd have to go off them on a yearly basis for a few months in order to see where I am – because there is no indication of when I'll actually go into full-blown menopause. It could be four months, or four years. There's just no telling, and since I don't have sisters...no help there.

Surgically, there's an ablation that could be done (I think it's called a hysteroscopy – where they go in vaginally). They can remove the fibroids via a laparoscopy, too – through a small incision near the belly button. Or they can go into my uterus through the veins in my groin to cauterize the blood vessels that are feeding the fibroids, which would at least cut off their blood supply. And the fourth option, of course, is a hysterectomy.

So.

She then proceeded to the physical exam. And the minute she put her hand on my abdomen, she said, "Oh wow." Um, okay.

Apparently, the reason I am wide when I turn sideways is because my uterus is huge. Or, as she put it, if I had come in to see her and I was twenty-five instead of fifty-two, she'd ask me if I were pregnant. Because to her, my body feels about 5 months pregnant. Let me repeat that. FIVE. MONTHS. PREGNANT.

Yeah. Knew it. Okay, but there's a bright spot – it's not fat! It's my fibroid-filled uterus making me look big. That's a plus, right? *Right?* Sigh.

So, the surgical options have narrowed because my uterus is so damned huge. (She didn't even see the need to do a vaginal ultrasound – she could feel it. And then, suddenly, so could I.)

Surgically, I could go with the cauterizing of the blood vessels in my uterus to cut off the fibroids. But this will not get rid of the fibroids – it will merely stop them from growing (which would be, I'll admit, a total blessing).

OR: I could go with the total abdominal hysterectomy (with a low bikini incision). My ovaries would be left in, because I don't have any family history of cancer at all and, according to the doc, our ovaries have an important role to play as we age. They don't know what it is, exactly, but it's important.

This last option would give me my figure back (such as it is). The medication options will help with the blood flow, but it won't shrink the fibroids into non-existence, from what I understand. (Even after menopause, the fibroids don't just go away, and I'll be my normal, slightly fist-sized uterus girl again. Oh, no. That, of course, would be too easy.)

When I told my husband, the first thing I did was help him feel my abdomen. Almost from hipbone to hipbone, from pubic bone to just below my belly button, my uterus fills my abdomen. Considering it's supposed to be roughly the size of my fist, it's beyond ginormous. I feel awkward, ugly, huge and impossible.

Tom, my love, wants me to do whatever will give me the best long-term health outcome. He doesn't care if I don't get my figure back. (I think a main part of it is he doesn't want me going in for any surgery, at all. I can totally understand that.) But me? I'm tired of feeling huge. Of being 5 months pregnant. I've been this way, steadily growing, for four years now. And I'm tired. Anemically tired.

I don't know what I'll end up doing. I've got research to do. The doc took a biopsy of the fibroids and we should get the results back in a few days. Then we'll sit down, the three of us, and figure out what our next step should be.

Why am I writing about this here? Because it didn't dawn on me that when a GP doc gave me an exam in 2010, that she might be wrong when she pressed on my uterus and said, "What's your bladder doing there?" I'll never know how different things might have been, if this had been caught in 2010.

Things change in our bodies as we women age, and we need to be alert to the changes. The Niagara Falls part of my period didn't really get bad until about 3-4 years ago. That should have been my first clue. But I wasn't paying any attention. I had assumed that everything was as it should be.

I was wrong. Learn from my mistakes. Pay attention to your health. It's important, and no one else can possibly do it for you.

Of course, I went in for the surgery. I was lucky to be able to pick a surgeon who does this kind of surgery a lot. He was also a Urologist, so knew how careful he needed to be.

(Note: my fibroids were calcified, so he had to do the low bikini incision. He also took a photo of my huge uterus after he removed it and showed that photo to my husband. Apparently, it was the largest calcified-fibroid uterus he'd ever seen.)

After six weeks of recovery, I felt so much better. SO much better. So, ladies. Don't skip your gynecologist appointments, even if you think you're far from childbearing age. It's not about that, at all.

The Menopause

I've been seeing a lot of emotional howling on Facebook from women in their forties about menopause. "Why didn't anyone tell us?" seems to be the cry. A part of me is dumbfounded. How can you women not know that you're going to go through menopause? Did you not watch Golden Girls?

There are books out there, you know. Do your research. Don't leave your health to the doctors, or to the whims of fate. If you don't have a copy of Susun S. Weed's book The New Menopausal Years, grab it. As it says on the cover, "for women 30 to 90." I first picked it up when I was in my thirties. Dr. Christiane Northrup is also a good resource for women's health issues.

Please. Stop howling on Facebook, ladies, and see to your own education. Become informed before you need it. And if you're already in peri-menopause, read read read!

About three months after my hysterectomy, my gynecologist put me on a hormone patch, and I finally stopped feeling like I was going to crawl out of my skin and flay alive everyone around me. I was on that patch for over a year, and then when I went to pick it up one month, the price had gone from $30 to $100 per month. I said nope, walked out of the pharmacy, and dropped the hormones cold turkey. Don't do that, either. That's not healthy, apparently, and I got scolded by my gynecologist. But she also didn't blame me, and as it turned out, the time I was on it was the time I most needed to be on it.

Writing this now, almost seven years after the fact, I can say that the patch took care of the worst of my menopausal symptoms. Your mileage may vary; no two women will have the same symptoms in the same way, and for the same timeframe. See your doctor. Read the books. Become informed.

Your family will thank you later.

Oh, and as a reminder...women have been going

through menopause for as long as women have lived long enough for their bodies to change. At least we, now, have ways to deal with it, both medically and naturally. Take advantage of what is available to you. Don't allow yourself to be blindsided by menopause.

And gents? Women aren't the only ones who go through bodily changes as we age. Start doing your own research, as well.

3

SHIFT NUMBER THREE

The third thing that happened to shift my life was the twentieth anniversary of my brother Scott Cunningham's death in March of 2013. I had just celebrated my fifty-third birthday that February. An age he didn't get to see.

Twenty fucking years. Would he still call me Legs if he were alive? I do know he'd probably have a home on one of the Hawai'ian Islands, and I'd have visited Hawai'i to catch up with him. I still haven't been to Hawai'i, but I'm hoping to go soon and honor him.

In 2013, I was working in a day job that wasn't horrible for a privately-held, extremely small company that did important work, and I was employee number eight. I was also the only woman (and soon I came to believe they didn't even think I was female. But that's another story). I got this job eight months after my brain surgery, and I was sporting a broken leg at the time. That said, I had a sense of humor, so did the guys interviewing me, and they ended up hiring me.

As I'm still there as of this original printing, I can't

complain. They treat me well; they gave me a place to recover, both mentally and physically, while getting paid. It helps me pay the bills while Tom works on his acting career. They, in turn, receive an employee who can handle almost anything they throw, so a win/win. Especially since I don't have meltdowns anymore trying to learn something new. That first year, though, phew. It was a tough one. I'm grateful they stuck with me.

2013. March. Scott's death anniversary. I'm still writing, but I'm restless. My sons are grown, though still living at home, and going to college. My publishing company wasn't asking for more books from me (though there was definitely a book 3!!!), and the company was starting to slide into obscurity. Heather Howland had left just after my first book had been published, to work with Liz Pelletier and start up Entangled Publishing. I felt adrift, like something was lacking in my life.

I saw an ad on Facebook for The Silva Method[1]. Increase my brain power? Learn to meditate? Become psychic? Sign me up!

I took the free seminar offered through Mindvalley[2], instead of their whole course, but it stirred something inside me. It took me out of myself and opened up my brain.

Of course, once they have your email address, they have you. I started receiving ads for all these interesting courses but couldn't quite give myself the permission to grow.

Oh.

Interesting, isn't it? I couldn't give myself permission to grow.

During 2013 and 2014, I was also the Chapter President of the Los Angeles Romance Authors chapter of Romance Writers of America. I was in my first leadership position. What I said, what I wrote for the chapter newsletter, affected people. It mattered. Writing this now makes me realize that I didn't completely know how much my words mattered. At the time, I just understood that I had work to do, people to energize and protect, and the words in the President's column in each monthly newsletter were poured out from my heart, touching other people.

Writing can be a tough business. Lonely. I fully believe I'm a writer due to my dad encouraging me to join RWA back in 2001 (I finally did in early 2002). That first year, in a dumpy building behind a mall in the San Fernando Valley, I found my first professional home. Those were my people, they spoke my language, and they were doing things I was doing, but better and faster. I had much to learn.

Romance writers, in general, are the most generous, the kindest, people in any professional organization. They help lift you up, instead of tear you down. They answer your questions, they critique your manuscript, they hold your hand while you hit send on a submission to an agent or an editor. The encouragement is paramount, because doubt so easily slips in to shred our confidence. Anyone who tells you that writing a romance novel is formulaic and easy, just laugh at them. It's anything but formulaic, anything but easy.

What's more important than writing happy endings for people to read who may be going through tough times?

The friends I have made in the romance writing industry are life-long heart friends. Some of them have become my closest friends, the ones I can confide my fears to, the ones who prop me up, kick me in the ass, and celebrate with me. Some of them are no longer with us, and I grieve the loss.

Despite not giving myself permission to grow, I was growing anyway merely by being in this leadership position.

In this same two-year timespan, I also made a connection with Boroughs Publishing, and received a four-book contract for the StarTide Agency series. Things were really going well, and I was excited about my career. I turned in the holiday novella, Christmas Star, to Chris Keeslar, at the time the Editor in Chief. When I finished Guarded Star, I turned that in to the editor who acquired me, Jill Limber.

Christmas Star was published in November of 2014, and Guarded Star in 2015. The other two in the series were published in 2016 with a different editor, but still with Boroughs.

I continued to feel a restlessness. A culture of hate was slowly taking hold of my country, and after my own bouts of hate and rage, I felt myself growing more compassionate, instead of less. I felt myself turning inward, and availed myself of many of Mindvalley's classes, which broadened my mind and sense of self.

Three years later, the hatred and anger in our world is more palpable than ever. Social media is a quagmire of opinions and blocking and shamefest after shamefest. It brings out the worst in people, I believe, having the ability to hide behind a keyboard and throw hate at others.

I have come to a realization this year. All that we have is ourselves. If we're lucky, we have people who love us and who we love. I don't care how old you are, or how young. I don't care if you are rich, or if you're poor. What I care about is how are you growing?

How are you making yourself mentally, physically, and emotionally invincible to the best of your ability? A fluid mind, a strong body, a loving heart. Do you have goals that others told you were ridiculous, and impossible? They can be yours. All of this can be yours, if you want it. If you're willing to work for it.

But! You say. I have physical limitations! Or, I live alone! Or, I'm poor! Or, I work three jobs!

It doesn't matter, dumpling.

The truth is, you can probably be physically stronger than you are right now. You just may have to get hella creative to figure out how to get stronger. But you know what? There's a ton of stuff online. Check it out. (There are always people who cannot get physically stronger, and to them I send love. The rest of us? Yeah, we can.)

You can eat healthier, too. Recipes? Online! (Pssst.... stop eating sugar. You'll feel much better. Trust me. Or don't. But do your research, don't take my word for it, and be careful where you put your money.)

You can broaden your understanding of anything that interests you. You just have to make that choice to learn.

Live alone? That doesn't mean you can't have an open and loving heart.

Limited income? The library. They have terrific resources. Not to mention all the free stuff on the internet.

Work three jobs? My heart goes out to you. I've got nothing...but you're smart. I bet you can figure it out if you want to.

Look. Life is a work in progress. I am fumbling about in the dark just as much as everyone else is, and if they say they aren't fumbling and scared at times, no matter how perfect their life may be, they're lying.

I'm not saying that life doesn't pose challenges unique to us; it does. Everyone's challenge is different. But to believe we are stuck and cannot change? That I will not accept. If you do, I'm gonna give you the side-eye.

We are who we are, in part, because of everything that

has brought us to now. If we want to change, we have to work at it. Change comes from within, from stepping off the well-beaten path we always walk and trying something new. Change comes from opening our minds up to possibilities we haven't, in the past, been able to even contemplate. Change comes from opening our hearts to others and viewing others with compassion. Giving ourselves that same loving compassion.

Having compassion and empathy for others is not a weakness. It is a strength that carries nations. It is a strength that lifts up others and makes life easier for all. Those who view compassion and empathy as weaknesses are those who are the most in need of compassion, for my guess is they have seen little of it in their lifetime and have become hard in response.

Don't be hard. Soften enough to reach out. Ask.

That said...truth time here. I'm not good at asking for help. I wasn't good at it before I had kids, and I'm not good at it now. When our kids were younger, I was lucky. My husband was there. Plus, we had neighbors who had kids who liked our kids, and they all got to know each other when they were very young. Somehow, it got easier to be a neighborhood family, if that makes sense.

For several years, we had each other's backs. In my forties, I often kept their kids during summer breaks because I could. I held summer school for them, so they'd remember simple math and how to make their cursive letters (this was when they were in second or third grade... the older kids I had write short stories, ha!).

They responded in kind by taking our kids for a week or so at a time when we took a couple of European vacations.

Then, too, one couple were both nurses. They have pulled splinters out from under my fingernails. They have offered me shoulders to cry on and wine to sip. A pool to cool off in. I got their son an interview at Coldwater Creek, and he got the job. We've shared many meals together, especially as our kids grew up.

Now we've grown apart, as our kids have grown apart. They still live around the corner from us, and I still cherish them, their son is my first third son (yeah, I have two third sons), but times have changed. I guess that's normal.

The thing is, even when I was bad at asking for help, I asked. If I can do it, so can you. And the more you ask when you truly need help, the easier it gets.

Growth lives just beyond your comfort zone.

Happy is as Happy Does...

What is your innate outlook on life? Are you inherently an optimist? Or do you always find the worm in the salsa? Are you living with your breath caught, just hoping the next minute won't punch you in the face? (If so, gods I'm sorry.)

What do you do for fun on a sunny weekend? Do you seek out the good in life? The funny? The joy?

What would your life look like if you looked for the joys in daily living?

Tom and I took our Whimsy pup for a walk today. We went to a park we don't usually take him to, and he spent almost the entire walk with his big fluffy tail tucked between his back legs.

He was so uncomfortable. Too many people he didn't know. So many smells he wasn't sure of. Anxiety rolled off him in waves.

Whimsy relaxed once we got back into the car, but when we stopped and walked him at a not-quite-open-yet mall, he freaked out again, tail between his legs. It wasn't until we got him home and he hopped out, saw the familiar driveway, that his tail popped back up.

He doesn't like new places.

People, too, often don't like going someplace new, physically, mentally, or emotionally. Many people don't like crowds, or spending time with other people they don't know. I get it, I do. But sometimes, getting out of your house will take you out of yourself. Sometimes seeing other people, talking to them, tasting new foods, can shake you out of your innate bias.

If you're lucky, you have someone in your life who will put their arm through yours and say, "Come on, let's go explore," and if you're smart, you'll go with them.

We are capable of growth at any age. Our hearts and minds can hold more ideas than you may believe. We can learn new things, we can have new experiences, and we can find new things to like and dislike. Nothing has to stay the way it is at this moment.

Actually, nothing WILL stay the way it is, but we won't notice the changes until they are beyond our ability to do anything about.

Don't you want to be the architect of your own story? Don't you want to fashion your life the way you want it?

There's nothing stopping you, except you.

Don't stop yourself. Too many other people are happy to do that for you. Psst...don't let them stop you, either.

Each of us chooses how we go about our day, whether we are aware of it or not. So, do yourself (and those around you) a favor.

Choose love.

Choose kindness.

Choose to keep a happy heart, in this increasingly bitter and angry world, seemingly overrun with bullies.

Look for the good, even if it may seem impossible to find.

Be a light for someone else. You never know when a kind word, or a smile, will change someone's life.

Sending you love, and long, tight, squishy, knees-to-shoulders, heart-to-heart hugs. The kind of hugs we all deserve, and so rarely receive.

4

PODCASTS, BOOKS, AND STRANGERS

My journey to this new place I'm in started at Mindvalley, back in 2013. After The Silva Method, I learned the 11 Forgotten Laws with Bob Proctor (The Law of Attraction is the 12th one); I learned to meditate with Emily Fletcher and The M Word. I learned to explore my mind with Jeffrey Allan. I took Instant Transformational Therapy with Marisa Peer, and learned Six Phase Meditation with Vishen Lakhiani.

In late-2016, I got healthy and lost weight with Wildfit[1] and Eric Edmeades, and then my dad died in early 2017, and I said fuck it to being healthy because my broken heart needed those martinis, damn it. I'm working to get back to healthy eating now. I've been doing 10 minutes of targeted exercise daily (use it or lose it is my new mantra as I head into my sixth decade). And I'm transitioning into a different exercise program soon, because variety is good. The dog is happy, because he's getting almost daily walks now.

In 2015, I bonded with a few friends via Mindvalley, and through their advice I was turned on to The Tim Ferriss Show, a podcast where Tim Ferriss[2] interviews top performers in just about any sport/business/artistic endeavor you can think of.

Suddenly, my drive into work consisted of listening to Tim talk to all these people who were driven, successful, in wildly different pursuits. I was introduced to a sex worker, to the man who created Tom's shoes, to Seth Godin (I know!), to Eric Ripert (the man behind the chef...a fascinating two-hour plus interview), LeBron James, Dita von Teese, and oh, so many more people. My world was expanding.

But the one thing that kept coming up, that he asked everyone, was...what is your morning routine?

Without fail, every single person had one. I don't remember them all, as that's a lot of podcasts, but I remember everyone had a morning routine, regularly waking up before the rest of their household.

Up until this year, my morning routine consisted of waking up, looking at the clock, and debating with myself as to whether I could sleep for another hour or so. I'm sure no one is surprised that I'm regularly late for work.

At any rate, this idea of a morning routine stuck in my brain as something I needed. But it took a class on writing that really wasn't a class on writing to nudge me further.

Becca Syme's[3] class, *Write Better Faster*, was more a psychological approach to how our brains worked and what type of person we were than a how-to-write class. Why try to be a plotter if you needed to be inside the story before you could work it out? (That's me...I'm an 'inside the story' kind of writer.) That's a horrible explanation of a wonderful class, and I apologize. Becca is also putting together a class called *Live Better Faster* for the non-writer. I highly suggest you check it out.

As I was coming off a dreadful fall/winter in 2018, full of box set publishing stress and overblown drama, taking

Becca's class in early 2019 allowed me to take a deep breath and relax about writing, publishing, publicizing, everything. I also drew back from some less than healthy online relationships, which helped. (I highly recommend the "unfollow" button.)

Becca's class reminded me that I'm only in competition with myself, not anyone else. That publishing schedule for 2019 that I had worked hard on in December, well, I let go of it. (Ten books in one year was a bit much, and way out of my capability at the time. I was told to dream big! I dreamed impossible, instead. Now, I'm dreaming intelligently. Um.?)

Becca had a list of books for us to read, if we wanted to deep dive into other areas of our life, and that is how I picked up Hal Elrod's The Miracle Morning. I read that in a couple of days, and added two more books to my rotation – The Miracle Equation by Hal Elrod, and Deep Work by Cal Newton. I also slipped The Power of Habit by Charles Duhig, and The Portable Carl Jung in there.

As time went on, and as I finished book after book, I added Earth Works: Ceremonies in Tower Time, by H. Byron Ballard; Joseph Campbell's Myths to Live By; Paganism, an Introduction to Earth-Centered Religions by Joyce & River Higginbotham; and other books (see listing in the Appendix).

What I read of Elrod's work was echoed in Duhig's work. Newton's work dovetailed with Elrod and Duhig. And Jung? He just sort of connected everything, as did Campbell.

I started with Elrod's formula for the morning. Get up, drink water, brush teeth, then do meditation, affirmation, visualization, exercise, reading, journaling. I naturally wake up between 5 and 5:30am, so if I actually GET up then, I have time to do everything. And if I don't, I have less time to spend on each activity. Elrod suggests a minute on each area (get the book – you know you want to) if you're tight for time. Trust me – a minute holding plank position isn't easy if you don't do it all the time!

(By the way, I'm not being sponsored by anyone that I mention here. No one has paid me money to push their work; I only share what I, personally, have found to have value. Your mileage may vary. The trick is to start exploring your options.)

Newton suggests the first hour of your morning be one of personal growth, so that dovetailed with Elrod. After a few days of doing things Elrod's way, I started to switch it up. Exercise came last, almost always, because – yeah.

During this time, I finished both The Miracle Equation by Elrod and Deep Work by Newton. (I'm still working on the Duhig and the Jung, though I have moved on to other books as well.) It may have taken me two-plus months to do it, but I can guarantee that I wouldn't have read them at all if I hadn't taken the time first thing in the morning to read three pages in one book and then three in the other book.

Then I downloaded the Mindvalley app onto my phone (I'm a yearly subscriber), and Robin Sharma popped up. I need to actually take the entire two- month course, but what I got from the couple of lessons I listened to was he likes to break up his morning into three twenty-minute sections. Twenty minutes of exercise, twenty minutes of reading, twenty minutes of meditation, in whatever order you please. But again, first thing in the morning. He's a big believer in the 5 O'clock Club. (For that matter, it seemed like everyone Tim Ferriss interviewed started their day between 4 and 5 a.m.)

So my mornings took a turn. I still begin with meditation, as I need to put heat on my eyes every morning anyway because of dry eye syndrome, and the two just seem to go together. After that, I put on my tennis shoes and do my ten minutes of targeted exercise (sometimes via Mindvalley. This isn't an ad for them, seriously – I get no kickbacks. They just have really good stuff). Or, you know, whatever other exercise thing has taken my fancy.

I'm not as fit as these kids in the videos are. My knees can't do what they can do, so I modify the exercises to fit my body. That said, I'm on the fourth week of a four-week plan now, and I'm happy to say I can hold a plank position for twenty seconds. Will this exercise routine change? Yes. (I can always return to yoga.) Actually, I've already started a longevity program that I have high hopes for keeping me healthy and spry into my golden years.

After exercise, I started working with Benebell Wen's[4] Spirit Keeper's Tarot, the 22-week course. Her plan had me focusing on something different each day of the week. Dense. Oh goodness, that course is dense. But so, so good. And...I found I couldn't keep up with it. It is intense, dense, packed with information and to-dos, and took more of my morning time than I was prepared to devote to it. So for now, it waits for me to return to it.

But this is when it really hit home for me. You don't have to follow anyone else's morning routine. You just need to *have* one and commit to it. Commit to yourself. Because of my morning routine, I am able to write in the mornings. That is, in part, how I finished this book, writing a thousand words at time after my morning routine and before breakfast. I also crammed words in at odd hours on the weekend, in a frenzy of too much coffee. Actually, that's how eighty percent of this book got done, but still...without my morning ritual, I might not ever have started the work. So there's that.

My morning routine fluctuates. Meditation is a given, as

is some form of exercise and writing. Some days I play with Zentangles, as I'd love to be an artistic sort but I'm kinda really not. Most mornings now I'm walking the dog for at least ten minutes, which he totally appreciates, and it gets me out of the house. Plus, I need my non-fiction reading time, and the early mornings seem to be the only time I have for that.

At any rate, I still get to work late, but at least now I have a solid sense of satisfaction. I've gotten some important work done each morning, including my exercise. Since I get in before the boss does, it's all good. So far, anyway.

There's a reason I'm hyping a morning routine, though. It's not just so you can get your dream goals accomplished, although yeah, that's one reason.

The other reason has everything to do with the world we currently inhabit, and what we can do to change things.

What could you do if you allowed yourself to think big? What could you do, if you believed that you could be an agent of change?

Your morning ritual is where you can expand your vision. Expand who you want to be, and practice that. Expand how you want your world to be and aim for that. Read in those areas you want to expand in your life.

You don't have to tell anyone what you're doing. You can keep it private. Or you can tell the world. It really doesn't matter, as long as you're doing it for you. If other people mock you? Let them. That just means they don't understand, and you're not obligated to enlighten them.

Let me say that again. *You are not obligated to enlighten anyone who mocks you as to your purpose.* Your purpose is not necessarily mine. Mine is not necessarily yours. And you know what? That's what makes the world turn. Embrace that.

5

MEET THE WORLD - READ A BOOK

It is my belief that people don't read enough. I know that for years, all my reading was entertainment reading. But entertainment reading, as I have finally come to realize, isn't enough. We need to read to understand, or travel to understand.

But travel can be expensive. Reading gives us a window to the world. The only problem is, most of us don't read widely. I'm a white woman. I tend to gravitate to those works that give me comfort, not the ones that shake me.

When Toni Morrison died recently, I was ashamed to realize I'd never read anything she'd written. I picked up the first couple of her books, and am now reading The Bluest Eye. Tom had never read her, either, and he's looking forward to reading them as well.

Oh, the poetry Ms. Morrison writes...her writing shakes me. Turns my world view sideways. And I am better for it.

My point is, we can allow ourselves to get shaken by what we read in the safety of our homes. We can allow ourselves to have experiences that we'd never otherwise get. Readers tend to be more empathetic, kinder people than those who don't read. Why? My guess is, because we're exposed to all kinds of people, good, bad, evil, clueless, and of every nationality (ideally).

In reading a book like The Power of Habit, we are introduced to the science of habit. Plus, reading to deepen our education in the sciences is important. Not because we are interested in working in those sciences or getting a degree in them, but because our innate curiosity is piqued. We need to know.

Unfortunately, that need to know, that curiosity, has somehow been stifled in this country. Snuffed out as surely as if a thick, wet fabric had landed on everyone's brains, blanketing out every curious thought we've ever had about anything.

What this world needs, in my opinion, is more people who read. More people who are willing to step out of their comfort zone and learn what it's like to be a young black girl who just wishes her eyes were blue, and her friend who is horrified that she can't see how beautiful she is, just as she is. (Toni Morrison, The Bluest Eye.)

We need more kindness. Kindness, however, starts with us. It starts with personal growth, of putting time into caring about the words we read, the thoughts we think, the beauty around us. Then we need to take that kindness, that thoughtfulness, out into the world and share it.

I don't know. Maybe I'm saying this wrong.

What would your life look like, if you fed yourself a steady stream of books and documentaries that took you out of your comfort zone? Would it make you kinder? Would it make you see others as equals?

Three pages a day. Two pages. One book at a time. One documentary at a time.

Now, if you take up my reading challenge, this means

you'll change. You'll have to, with all the new information flooding your brain circuitry. I've changed since January 2019, and I like to think it's for the better. The thing is, not everyone around you will want you to change. Not everyone will encourage you to change. You see, if you change, that means those who love you will change.

Or maybe they won't, and you won't like what you see in them. Because maybe they're scared, that you're going someplace they can't, or won't, go.

Fear. Change scares people. When we change, even if it's a slow change, those who love us can get antsy. What are we going to demand of them, if we change? Will we want them to get up with us at five in the morning? Will we want them to read literature outside their comfort zone? Will we ask them to be compassionate?

I love my silent mornings. I love it when I'm the only one up and getting things done. When my husband gets up with me, it's a rarity, and I have to just smile and do my morning routine without letting him distract me. Not an easy thing!

That said, I am not a slave to my morning routine. There are times when he pulls me into his arms, back into the warmth of our bed, and I'd be a fool to turn away and say, "No, gotta meditate." Right? I mean, come on now.

There are times when I'm sick. Or hungover. Or I oversleep and need to rush out the door and just don't want to take the time to go through my routine. I've found that it's just fine, and you know why?

My days always go better when I put in my morning routine of growth. Always. When I don't get that time in the mornings, I feel all out of sync with myself, as well as the rest of the world. Which is why the next morning, I'm back at it. It's hardwired into me at this point.

I wish I could tell you that my morning routine has

made my willpower iron-clad, but it hasn't. And you know what? That's okay.

You will wake up on a Saturday at 5am, look at the clock, and roll over and go back to sleep. You will go places via airplane (vacation, business, family issues, whatnot), and maybe not have the ability to do your morning ritual. Or someone close to you will die, and you'll feel like dying with them, and you won't do your morning ritual. You know what? That's normal.

Every time I don't do my morning ritual, for whatever reason, I miss it. I strive to get back to it the next morning. When I travel, it often takes me two days to get back to it after any plane trip. That's life. That's okay. That's normal.

That's also when you know it works, when you realize that you miss it. When you miss the mental and physical stimulation. When you miss that sense of satisfaction of having done awesome work while everyone else is sleeping.

That's why, the next morning, you'll go back to your morning routine. Yes, it's that important. Don't start your day with the intention to just get through it. Set your intentions in a mindful way for your upcoming day. Get a jump on it, so you're ready when the next opportunity comes.

Do you want more out of your life? If so, your morning is where you can grab for it. Work for it. That part of the day where no one else is up, you can move through your morning in silence as you do the important work that no one else but you can do.

You've got this. And I've got your back.

6

BROKEN

There are people out there who believe they are broken beyond repair. That their spirit, and their heart, and their ability to trust, is broken. Shattered into a million pieces.

I believe that people can feel broken, absolutely. But I also believe in the resiliency of the human spirit, and that with the right circumstances around them, the right friendships, those broken people can heal and flower and grow to be strong, lovely and loving, and amazing people who are no longer bitter, afraid, alone.

Often, however, this means the broken ones need to turn their backs on their past in order to face a happier future. This could mean breaking off unhealthy relationships, walking away from so-called friends, or even cutting family ties. Sometimes, we need to let go of rigid rules we've chosen to live by, because we can finally recognize they are unhealthy rules. The simplest thing first is to figure out what's toxic in your life and what you need to cut loose.

Doing it, cutting those ties, isn't simple. But if you're one who considers themselves broken, feel my hand in yours.

Search for other people who will lift you up rather than step on you. People who will give you truth simply and without fuss. People who will love you and protect you and defend you and let you find your joy.

They are out there. I swear it.

I am lucky, I admit it. I've never felt, or been, totally broken and alone. But I have known those people, and I have seen amazing transformations in them when they decide to deep dive into their lives and work on their personal growth. Whether by the practice of forgiveness, meditation, reading widely, yoga, eating healthier, or just reaching out to a therapist, changes can be made.

The Universe wants you to succeed and be joyful. I do, too.

My nickname in second grade, given to me by one of my classmates, was "Little Miss Perfect." (Say it in a sneering voice, please.) I didn't realize, for the longest time, that it was a negative. I always tried hard to be perfect. I worked diligently at school. I kept my hands clean. I didn't always have the right answer when called on, but I could read out loud in a clear voice.

My quest for perfection didn't stop in second grade. It followed me throughout my life (though I was never a straight A student). I hated being wrong, about anything. I hated making mistakes. I thought for sure the world would stop turning if I weren't perfect, always. I needed to be right, about everything.

I don't remember when I gave up the quest for perfection, the need to be right, but I'm pretty sure it was sometime after I had children. No, that was the last gasp of my perfectionism...it was before that.

Sometime during the first decade of our marriage, Tom repeatedly demonstrated what I needed to learn...when he was wrong, he said so, and life moved on. He learned. (He also said it was the best way to end an argument.)

What a revelation. One that I had to experience, over and over again.

In my twenties, when I was working in a large computer company that has since gotten swallowed by IBM, I still had that drive to be perfect. But I messed up. Quite a bit, actually. But through Tom's ongoing example, I quickly learned to admit when I had made a mistake.

And the world did not stop.

Often, all the Universe wants is for us to admit when we're wrong, when we've made a mistake (especially in our relationships), so we can heal wounds, carry forward, and do our best not to make that mistake again. It's when we don't admit it that we get hit, over and over, with making that same error, time and time again.

My lovelies. We were not put here on earth to be perfect. We were not put here to strive for perfection. We are here to learn, and to love.

We will make mistakes. We will learn and grow from our mistakes, if we can admit we made them. We need to be able to go face to face with our boss, our dear friend, our spouse, our child, and say, "I was wrong. I made a mistake." Maybe add an "I'm sorry" in there, too.

We need to be able to do that without feeling shame, or anxiety, or fear. There is nothing wrong with admitting you were wrong. There is nothing wrong with growing.

There is nothing wrong with being human, that perfectly imperfect person that is you.

There are days when it seems all of social media is full of people who feel like they're failing at life. That they can't catch a break. That they can't "adult", no one showed them how, they'll never get it right, and they're full of despair. The systems are rigged against them (especially in health care – I see this all the time and it both breaks my heart and infuriates me).

Sometimes those people are ones I know and cherish. But if I were to say these words to them directly, they wouldn't be able to hear me. So that's when I take to Facebook, to sort out my thoughts, and hopefully to give love and compassion and a helping hand to not only my close friends, but to those others out there who are exhausted by what life is handing to them. Sometimes it helps. Sometimes it doesn't. This post, below, is one of those.

March 22, 2016

Dear Hearts,

You are doing the best you can under the circumstances. Many of us are floundering at this adult thing, at this being a good parent, at being a good friend or lover, at being a good daughter/son to our aging parents, or at figuring out where and when to draw boundaries to protect ourselves. We're tapdancing frantically in our brains while we try to keep all the balls we're juggling up in the air.

You are not alone, even if it may feel like it. There are people who love you who are willing to lend a hand. But you know what? You need to ask for help. And for so many of us, that's difficult, if not impossible.

Don't let your ego win. Everyone needs help at some point or another. Today maybe it's you. Tomorrow it may be your neighbor. Whether it's a quick run to pick up one of your kids while you handle the other one, or whether it's a shoulder to cry on, ask.

The most important thing to remember is that, right now, this place you're in? You won't be there forever. It will be a memory at one point. Breathe, my lovelies. Treat yourself with compassion as you untangle this current knot in your life.

And ask. Let those of us who love you help out, if there's anything we can possibly do to lighten your load. Because trust me, at some point, we'll be the ones asking you for help. That's kind of the way this friendship thing is supposed to go. You know?

Sending you love, and daisies, and a big ol' hug.

7

EVERYONE'S SCARED

With the upheaval in America today, and fake news, and protections for all people, not to mention the land, the air quality, and the water quality protections being rolled back; with the instability in charge, everyone is scared (or they've closed their eyes).

When people are scared, they get ugly. My way or the highway. Your opinion has no validity. Screaming matches on Facebook, Twitter, and in person are numbing us to who we really are, and who our neighbors, friends, and relatives really are. I had one relative block me. Another I had to block. My admittedly distant love toward them (because I'd never met one, and the other I last saw when I was a small child) could not overcome their fear and hatred of my beliefs.

The ugliness that people post is horrifying. The corruption in our government is horrifying. Each day brings a new outrage to the point where we find ourselves growing numb from it all. It's an exhausting layer on top of our already exhausting lives.

The following is a Facebook post I put up when I finally had had enough, when my thoughts finally had coalesced enough to put it down into words.

August 3, 2019

So here you go, from my heart to yours.

Treat each other gently. Even those on the "other side" of any given position. Most of the time people are acting out of fear or hurt or anger. Most of the time people are going through one variation of hell or another, and don't bother to tell anyone.

Most of the time, most of the people that you see on the street are in a world of physical, mental, and/or emotional agony you know nothing about. Or they are dead inside, even with the outward trappings of success/money/relationships.

Most of the time the people that make inflammatory comments on FB or Twitter are just crying out for attention...even if its negative attention...because they are in a space where they don't feel worthy of attention. Don't feel worthy of love.

I get it. We all want to spit back at those spewing venom against "our side" of things.

But that doesn't, ever, change anyone's mind.

Don't get me wrong. I'm not saying stick your head in the sand and pretend that life is lollipops and roses. I'm not saying be positive just to be positive.

Living a lie hurts. Feeling unloved hurts. Having a chronic illness is a debilitating hurt that tears at the very core of who we are as a person. How many people do we know who are going through absolute hell?

Maybe more than we're aware of. And maybe that's where those negative feelings and actions are coming from, maybe that's where the venom comes into play.

What can you do to change the status quo? Is it one calm conversation? A telephone call to a political figure? Donating to a charity, of perhaps your time more than your money? Is it becoming politically active, and running for local office? Is it, perhaps, reaching out to your chronically ill friend, and asking what you can do to help them that day? I don't care what you do, nor do I necessarily want to know what you do. But for your own sake, for your own heart and soul, do something.

Be the change. See the person behind the behavior. Let go of those people and actions and habits that no longer serve you and turn to what will ultimately serve both you and the highest good. Because more change is in the wind, and it's a cold change, one without heart.

All we have is each other. We come from Spirit and shall return to Spirit...but what we do while we're here matters. Never forget that.

It's looking dark, I'm not gonna lie. Neither am I going to elucidate – if you're curious, check the real news outlets. Things are shady and have been for a long time. How are we to survive?

I'm not so concerned for me as I am my sons. They aren't mated yet, so no grandchildren, which a part of me is deeply grateful for because I don't think my heart could stand welcoming a baby of my blood into this time and place.

Though the children are our hope. Right? Every generation thinks that. I think we have to, because we keep messing up.

8

WEAR THE PEARLS

Seize the Day. Live!

This post is rather self-explanatory, but I'll explain anyway. I was coming off the hardest year of my life so far. My father – my first love, my rock, the man I loved more than any other on this planet, died in March of 2017, and all I had worked for health-wise and writing-wise just kind of slid off my radar. I felt adrift as my brother Greg and I went through all the motions one goes through when a parent dies, spending weekends at the house going through papers, dealing with banks, getting the house ready to sell. Dealing with the caregiver.

We sifted through the books and papers of daddy's life – he kept everything, every letter from a publisher, every bit of correspondence, so it was both wonderful and time consuming to go through. Much of it we simply put into a box to sort out later. But it was so hard. Those nine months were grief-filled. Yes, there was love, and joy, laughter with the tears, and writing of words. My heart was uplifted when I was able to spend time with my great-nephew Jackson, just a baby. Holding him, breathing in his sweet baby scent, helped me heal. The truth remains, however...it was a rough time.

So, this post is me, talking to me. It's my wake-up call to myself, to get myself moving. A reminder that life is out there, and to greet it with a wide-open heart and open arms.

Of all the posts I've ever written on Facebook in the past nine years, this one is probably the most shared of them all. This is the post that had people (especially Sylvie Fox, who wrote the Foreword) urging me to write this book.

January 1, 2018

Wear the pearls.

I mean it.

Wear the pearls, the negligee that has to be dry-cleaned, the lipstick that costs more than a good porterhouse steak. Wear the hell out of them and enjoy.

A few weeks ago, I was going through my drawers, cleaning things out because I wanted to start the new year a little more organized than I had been. I found jewelry that I had hidden away.

I found not only the pearls that my dad gave my mom, including the necklace he gave her as a wedding present (bought in Japan when he was there during the Korean War), the diamond and pearl earrings and the pearl bracelet that came later in their relationship; but also the pearls my husband gave me our third (or maybe fourth) married Christmas together.

And it struck me...I don't remember my mother wearing the pearls. I mean, maybe for my wedding...maybe for my brother's wedding...but not really, if that makes sense. Not only that, but I couldn't remember the last time I had worn my pearls.

When I looked at the pearls, my mom's and mine, in

their cases, it hit me that not wearing the pearls was tantamount to putting life aside...putting life on hold.

I've had that string of pearls from my husband for thirty-plus years and could count on one hand the number of times I'd worn them. And I realized that was totally fucked. What was I saving them for?

So, I wore them while I did some major cleaning out of stuff. I brought them on vacation with us, and I wore them at every opportunity.

Today, as I was going through boxes of my dad's life, Tom said to me, "This calls for pearls," and I realized he was right.

Tonight, I went to the grocery store. I had on black polka dot jammie pants, a flag t-shirt that's ripped across the chest, a red and blue plaid shirt, neon-pink shoes, and a raspberry beret. And my pearls.

Maybe it's because I'm in my late fifties and no longer give a fuck, but I felt beautiful in my pearls and plaid.

Wear the pearls. Wear the silk lingerie. Drink the good wine, let the sports car go fast on an open road. Don't wait until life is perfect...make it perfect by action.

Happy New Year, my loves. Happy New Year.

When I re-read the above, I realized something that I knew, but hadn't verbalized yet.

When my daddy died, and as we were getting the house ready for sale, I scoured his kitchen for china, and got the only pieces left of my maternal grandmother's china. I have a dinner plate, a salad plate, a cup and saucer. Of those four pieces, I've included the salad and dinner plates into my eclectic rotation of plates (which includes my parents' college commemorative plates).

My mom's grandmother's plates are a light pinkish color, maybe a salmon-y color (but natural, not color-added salmon, lol), with a silver rim. They'd been hidden away high up above my mother's oven for decades before I got them. Never used.

I realized that I needed to use them. I mean, come on. When I die, and my kids look at what I never use, will they even know or care that those pieces came from my mom's mom's mom? No. (I have sons who aren't interested in dinnerware other than what may be on top of such dinnerware for them to consume. I'm okay with this.)

Two-plus years on, every time I use one of those plates I smile. I notice, as well, that the silver edging is almost gone, because I do put them in the dishwasher.

I'm totally okay with this. You know why? After I'm gone, no one will care.

Use your cherished possessions. If no one after you will cherish them, what are you saving them for?

And if you have a child, a grandchild, a niece or nephew who might cherish one of your precious items, why not gift that relative while you are still alive? They will cherish it even more if you do so.

I had dolls that my grandmother Hazel Cunningham made for me when I was young. Ceramic faces, hands and feet, and beautiful hand-made dresses. They hung on my walls in my childhood and into my teens, and when I married, I wrapped them up and put them in my cedar chest.

Then I had sons. When my nephew and his wife had a daughter, I ended up giving the dolls to her (perhaps later than I should have). Quilts and quilt tops were given, as well.

I don't miss the dolls, and I am grateful that they have gone to family. My great-niece, a Cunningham, has the dolls that great-grandmother Hazel Cunningham made for me. It's a nice bit of continuity. But as she received them when she was beyond the doll-playing age, I hope that at least they grace her bedroom walls, and that she feels that family connection. Of course, now she's headed to college, so perhaps those dolls are tucked away for her children-to-be.

As for the quilt tops, there were so many that I felt no guilt or regret about passing several of them on to my nephew and his wife. I have two quilts that my grandmother Hazel made for me, and several tops that I need to have finished. Maybe someday, when I slow down and the pull of sitting and hand-quilting, the peace of it, tugs at me...maybe then I'll get the quilt tops out and get to work.

9

IF I COULD DO JUST ONE THING...

This is another post where the lack of compassion I found on social media both astounded and saddened me. Even people who I know are loving and compassionate can come across as hard and indifferent on social media. I know it's a defense mechanism, but it is so frustrating to see people misrepresent themselves, especially when they aren't aware of doing so.

The post directly following this one kept the garden theme, which is why I stuck it where I did.

As an aside...be careful which hill you decide to plant your flag on. Do you really need people to know you prefer Peets to Starbucks, or that you hate pumpkin spice (for instance)? Because frankly, no one cares. Sorry, but it's true.

July 9, 2019

A couple days ago, I found and re-read my mother's copy of The Secret Garden, by Frances Hodgson Burnett. You know, the story of two peevish young people, basically neglected by the ones who were supposed to care for them, who then find each other. As well as the hearty country lad (and his mother) who shows them how to grow things in the secret garden, one that had lain dormant behind a locked door for a decade.

The message of the book, to me, is that when we hug our ills, fears, sorrows, and complaints tightly to ourselves, when we pay attention to them over all else, when we let fear rule us, we remain peevish, unhappy people.

But when we turn outward, when we look to others, and get excited about growing things like plants and animals and ideas and dreams; when we breathe fresh air, run around in the sun, eat good food, and work to help things grow, when we have an eagerness to learn, we, too, grow. We grow healthier, happier, more resilient as our minds and hearts and bodies grow strong.

See, I think that's a part of what's wrong with the world today. People cling to slights and insults; they cling to their "my way or the highway" attitude on everything from religion to politics and which grocery store or shoe company or type of ice cream is "best." They pull themselves away from learning and feast on their own ills and beliefs anchored in stone, letting rancor eat away at their brains until there is no way any rationality will get through to them.

We all, collectively, are in need of getting out into the garden (so to speak), of believing in the Magic of Life - the Magic of exercise for a purpose, such as gardening; the Magic of good food, good friends, something worthwhile to do, and healthy laughter.

We are all human, all of us, no matter skin color, native language, or which continent we live on; and as such, we are all deserving of the rights and joys of life that, too often, people want to keep for themselves instead of sharing those rights, those joys (for the ills and sorrows will find us, whether we will or no).

If I could do one thing, make one impact on the world, it would be this...to point people's attention outward, away from their own ills and insults and aggravations and petty insecurities, and toward other people who just need encouragement, a little room to breathe, a little water, a little food, and lots of compassion; and then I would nudge them to give what they could toward making the world a better place. One garden, one ridiculously exciting idea, one child, one struggling adult at a time.

If I could only do this one thing, I would count myself blessed.

10-17-2015

Hope can be found in a garden. For what gardener ever planted seeds that did not hope to harvest from the grown plant?

This morning, I planted seeds. Thyme and sugar snow peas. The spinach Tom planted last weekend has already started coming up, and the lettuces too are showing some green. Where I live in southern California, autumn does not mean the garden settles down for a winter nap and an eventual snow blanket. Instead, we plant seeds and pray for rain.

When you are running low on hope, set foot in a garden. If you can, get dirt under your nails as you turn the soil. Plant a seed.

Plant perennials. Plant fruit trees that take years to bear fruit. Plant roses, to give to your loved ones when they bloom.

Be radical, and plant food plants. Kale and Swiss chard do well in my area. Artichokes, too, and man are the artichoke plants hard to kill. Plant a fig tree, or a citrus tree in your front yard, and put a sign up for your neighbors and passersby to help themselves. If you live in the Pacific

Northwest, plant berries in areas where others can access them. Spread the bounty, because a plucked plum or fig may give a passerby a dessert they hadn't expected or counted on, and isn't that a lovely way to show love?

If you can get them to grow, plant avocados (they like lots of water). A neighbor of ours has them along the side of their house, outside the fence, for any passerby to pick. Along with a plum tree and an apple tree that hangs over said fence. We've been grateful for those gifts, especially during lean times, over the years.

Check what is a good grower in your climate, and plant that.

Not only is it good for the environment, but gardening is good exercise. It forces you to go out and tend the land, which is always a positive.

10

TIME MANAGEMENT AND BEYOND

"I have observed that a life directed to an aim is in general better, richer, and healthier than an aimless one, and that it is better to go forward with the stream rather than backwards against it."
- Carl Jung

It's easy to get into the habit of being unhealthy. It's easy to let ourselves down, and be comfortable doing so. It is so easy to judge other people, to put our keen eye of observation on all that goes on around us. And yet, it is so difficult to scrutinize our own behavior, to see where we are harming ourselves thoughtlessly and habitually. This is another post where I am talking to myself, and it seemed to resonate with others, as well.

July 3, 2019

I've been making a lot of small, bad decisions lately. As I've been going about my day today, I'm mulling over the things I want to do...and I realized that the weight of my own expectations is sending me running back to comfort, rather than toward the pain of growth.

That realization stopped me in my tracks. I paused.

Stared out the window at work and sat with my massive discomfort.

I've started two online courses and have fallen behind. Oh, wait, plus there's that one from earlier this year - so make that three. No...damn it. Four. Sigh.

I want to do a deep dive into tarot practice...but thinking about it makes that sense of drowning rise up stronger.

Not to mention the whole eating poorly (because it makes me feel terrible) and drinking too much wine at night. Sigh.

My mission is my non-negotiable...and that's due at the end of July. And while that IS progressing, I'm still uncomfortable with all of it, having difficulty still in believing in myself and this new path. (By the way, got that one done.)

I take a breath. Then another. I can only do what I can do in a day. The first thing? I need to stop making small bad decisions, because those add up.

Shenpa[1]. Once I realized I was caught in the pain, I paused. I have two paths I can take. One, zooming down the small bad decisions path. Or two, take steps toward my discomfort until that becomes comfortable. Then set more missions beyond my comfort zone, and repeat.

I'm sure this will be a daily lesson...but I am learning.

That post was due, in part, because I'd let my morning ritual fray a bit. I'd become okay with having an unfocused morning, which led to a lot of other unfocused choices.

Do you see how a daily morning ritual can come in handy? It got me back on track. At some point, when I'm ready, I will go back to those online classes I paid for and didn't finish. I will build that time into my morning routine. It may take me longer to get through them, but they're on the list. At some point, they'll become imperative for me to work through, and I will. My need for those classes hasn't gone away; but my priorities shifted and will undoubtedly shift again.

That's just life, my friends. When you are struggling to complete something and feel further and further behind everyone else and feel like you're drowning in your to-do list, stop and take stock of what else is happening in your life.

Maybe that course is something that can wait, or maybe it's a necessity to finish off schooling, or is something for your job that really can't wait. Shift your priorities, do the thing, and not do something else if you're truly overwhelmed.

Do what is important for your life; don't force yourself to finish something just for the sake of finishing it, if in doing so you will stress yourself far beyond what is necessary.

Of course, I'm not talking about the serial unfinishers out there, those people who start writing a novel and never complete it; or who start a knitting/crocheting/quilting project and never finish it. Those who start creating a garden and never finish it, etc etc etc. That's a real thing, and I'm not talking about those people. I can't help you if you are a serial unfinisher. You probably need a therapist. Or maybe not. I don't know, I'm not a professional.

But if you're a person who is tougher on yourself than anyone else, if you feel you MUST DO ALL THE THINGS, then maybe cut yourself some slack. As we get older, we need to be a bit more selective on where we put our attention, don't you think?

As my dear friend Sara[2] says, time is the only thing we

don't get more of. And please, please stop comparing your workload with other people's workload. Stop comparing your success to other people's success. Let the only race you are in be with yourself. Are you doing better today than yesterday? Let that be your guide.

As I was reading all these personal growth books, I kept tripping over the same sound bites that seem really cool, but don't have much real meaning behind them. The below post is me talking to me again, sounding out the meanings behind these pithy quotes that many of us repeat to each other without really having a clue as to what they mean.

This post helped remind me to anchor myself when I come across these quotes, or others like them.

June 28, 2019

There are all these nifty sound bites in the personal growth industry - how you do anything is how you do everything - you can't have something different until you do something different - a goal without a plan is a wish - and they all sound really good, but can leave you floundering because there's nothing tangible to grasp.

From my reading, I have learned that it all comes down to the habit of consistency, how you talk to yourself, and the words you use. So, to take the last sound bite and make it tangible for me...

I am choosing to focus on one mission at a time. In so focusing, I have a process I use to get it done, which is I schedule time every day to work on it in the morning, after my morning ritual is complete. My scheduled time is protected. I commit to that time, in order to complete my mission on deadline and in good order. A tip - I do NOT pick up my phone, or go online, until my work on the mission for that day is complete.

Instead of "goal," I use mission. Instead of "plan," I use process. And above all, I schedule my time...and the mission comes first, before I go about the rest of my day.

This also is the tangible for the second sound bite - by tackling my mission in the morning, after my morning ritual, I am doing something different. By focusing on one mission until it's complete, I am doing something that I haven't done before. I am on the path of having something different, because I am doing something different.

As far as how you do anything is how you do everything...by focusing, by doing something different, by looking at my day and realizing how I can switch around when I do things for maximum progress, I am able to take that focus and apply it to other areas of my life.

What mission/goal have you always wanted to accomplish? How can you get there from here? I hope this gives you some ideas to start. Your time is precious. Spend it wisely.

11

ILLNESS

Life happens. Illness happens, whether it be yours or a family member where you are called upon to be caretaker. We fall behind where we want to be. Our brains become numb due to the drugs we're taking to manage our illnesses (however simple or severe), or due to the lack of sleep we're getting because of our care- taking.

Please, if you are walking this path either way (as a patient or as a caretaker), remember to be kind to yourself.

You are not your illness. Your brain will clear, and you will be able to handle the new tasks before you as you heal.

You are not your patient's illness. You deserve rest as well, and as your loved one heals, you will find your own strength again.

It may feel that life has passed you by during this interval. But trust me, it hasn't. Life is waiting for you to take back up the reins, and ride hard toward your desires.

This post was written because a couple of my dear friends were down with the upper respiratory infection from hell that took eight weeks and three different medications to clear up. I later had that same infection.

However. There are those who will never heal fully. There are those who are on a path of illness that cannot be course-corrected, and they will always have that illness/handicap/health issue. I was told in private, after I put this up, that perhaps this post was being insensitive to those people, and that maybe I should take it down.

Coming across this post here again, I hesitated. Does it strike a false note? I hope not. I watched my mother battle Multiple Sclerosis for fifty years. I watched my dad be her caregiver, until his age made that impossible.

I know that everyone's journey is not mine. I know that there are people who live daily with pain. I also know that there are people out there who do not let their illness define them, and who continue on to accomplish great things.

I guess what I'm truly saying here, is to be compassionate with yourself, whether you're the caregiver, or the one who needs the care. We all have good days and bad days. Days where we feel strong, and days where we need to just be.

I'm reminded of the cartoon (and I don't remember who it was by, forgive me) of two rats, sitting at a bar, beer in front of them. One rat is caught in a rat trap. The other rat says something to the effect of, well, your problems are more obvious than mine.

Some people's issues are more obvious, while others' issues are hidden. So I guess I should leave you with, be compassionate to all. I know I say this a lot – but you don't know what battles other people are facing.

12

BUT THOSE OBSTACLES!

There are always obstacles to your heart's desires. Some people prefer the obstacles to the success, because to overcome those obstacles, those boulders blocking the path, they have to grow. They have to change. And not everyone wants to change. Not everyone has the driving need to better their circumstances. This post is not for those people who don't want to change and grow; or maybe more accurately, those who don't see the need for change and growth.

This is for the rest of us who feel that there is more to reach for, more experiences to have, more joy to spread, more love to share. This post is for the dreamers who are also doers.

June 4, 2019

Every obstacle to success can be broken down into parts. Every part can be broken down again into subparts. Every subpart has an answer. There is nothing that cannot be worked out unless you decide to give up.

Everyone has feelings of doubt. Everyone has stared up

at the dark ceiling at three in the morning and wondered just what the fuck they thought they were doing with their life.

Self-doubts. Imposter Syndrome. One small issue leading to a bigger and bigger issue that we hide from, and then all the problems fester and grow so big we lack the stamina to deal with them.

You are not merely holding the worth of your personal successes. You, my friend, are holding the worth of every experience you've ever had, every love you've ever loved, every song you've sung, book you've read, or movie you've watched. You hold the worth of every sunrise or sunset that has taken your breath. You hold the worth of every tear you've cried, every pain you've healed. You hold the worth of everyone who has ever loved you, laughed with you, wished they were you.

You are the moon and the stars, and the earth beneath your feet. You are one part of the many hearts that beat across the world as they work, love, laugh, sweat, fight, pray, live, and die. You hold the glory of the ocean, the majesty of the mountains, the sweetness of birdsong, the beauty in a rose, and the austereness of the desert deep inside you.

You are meant to give your heart and soul to this life, holding nothing back for the future. Let me take your hand and guide you back to yourself, one step at a time.

Every obstacle to success can be broken down into parts. Every part can be broken down again into subparts. Every subpart has an answer.

There is nothing that cannot be worked out.

Until there is; and when you cannot work something out, when you cannot change something, accept it. Following is a lesson I learned from Hal Elrod and his book

The Miracle Equation, where he talks about The Five-Minute Rule. The Five-Minute Rule is where you're allowed to be angry, pissed off, feel whatever feeling you most need to feel about whatever bomb the world has tossed at you. Five minutes, tops. Then accept it.

Why? Because whatever happened, happened. It's now in the past. You can't change the past. If you hold onto the anger, the pain, helplessness, etc, all you're doing is keeping yourself angry and in pain. Acceptance is the key to moving forward, through those feelings. I'm not saying you have to like what happened. But as you cannot change the past, your way through is by accepting what happened.

May 23, 2019

Aim for a state of peace. There are so many things in this greater world, as well as personally, that we cannot change. Once we accept this, it is easier to move into our life with serenity.

I cannot change the fact that both my parents are dead, that my brother is dead, grandparents, aunts and uncles, all gone. I can only accept it. I cannot change the circumstances around my father the last few years of his life; I can only accept it. Not accepting what we cannot change leads to pain, sometimes depression.

We all have a choice. We can live in emotional pain over things that we cannot change, or we can accept them and gain a measure of peace.

I am not, of course, talking societal ills here. Those can and should and hopefully will change. But personal issues? Wrongs people have done you, past hurts, those things cannot change because they are in the past. When new pains/wrongs/hurt feelings/illnesses crop up, things that also can't be changed, allow yourself five minutes to rage, or cry, or feel all the feelings...time yourself, give yourself five minutes. Then accept it.

Always ask yourself...can it be changed? If you can't change it, accept it.

You'll save yourself a lot of pain that way and find yourself dwelling in peace more often than not.

Search out the beauty in life today. Search out and see the good things. Let the petty crises of the day pass you by. Be the best you that you can possibly be.

Sending you love, and light, and laughter...and most of all, acceptance.

August 22, 2018

We all get behind. Either in reaching out to friends, or in cleaning, or in remembering to pay bills, or a myriad of other things. Life is distracting. Life is messy and loud and beautiful and painful and sometimes so damned hard.

The trick to getting ahead isn't more to-do lists. It's not a stricter adherence to a routine - any routine, of any kind. It's not setting reminders or posting notes to your mirror which doesn't work anyway, on those days you forget to look in the mirror.

The way past it is to forgive yourself. Do what you can when you can. Make an effort to do more on days when you feel good and cut yourself some slack on those days you're not well. Be good to yourself.

That also means, know when you're procrastinating. Kick it to the curb, fifteen minutes at a time. Don't pamper yourself "just because," especially if that "just because" becomes a daily thing. There's a difference between being good to yourself and being overly indulgent. You know this.

This life thing. It takes guts, determination, an open heart, a lively sense of humor, compassion, mental agility, a willingness to be wrong, and a whole bunch of other things.

But you know what? I'd rather be here, even in these "interesting times," than be anywhere else.

So above all, be here, now. Don't wish today gone in favor of a perfect tomorrow that may never arrive.

The above, obviously, was written before I had found my morning ritual to be so, so important. However, it's true. Being stricter with yourself when you're overwhelmed isn't going to help. What will help, however, is a gentleness combined with structure.

You are important to many of those around you, both in real life and virtually. Never think otherwise.

If you need help, ask for help. I know I keep harping on this, but I believe it is important. Self-reliance is a necessary trait; but knowing when to ask for help when you need it is also a necessary trait.

Maybe get to know your neighbors, because in the times we currently live in? It may be your neighbors who save your life. Go beyond politics, skin color, language, and see the people around you. Don't ask them who they voted for, ask them instead about their childhood. Their families. How they grew up. Ask them about their favorite recipes, and maybe have a neighborhood picnic where everyone brings a favorite, with copies to share.

We are too complacent, thinking disaster of a political nature can't happen to us where we live. It can. It absolutely can. Think wider than your social circle. Think closer to home. If ICE walks the street, pounding on doors and looking for immigrants, will you save a neighbor? Will they save you?

If a neighbor's children are left behind because their

parents have been taken away, will you take them in, give them shelter?

These are interesting times, indeed. What are you willing to do? What is the line in the sand that you will not, absolutely will not, cross?

And are you prepared to take a stand? Most of us aren't.

13

CHANGE IS THE CONSTANT

April 29, 2019

The energy of Spring is coursing through me, through my life. I am so very grateful for all that I have been given, for all that I have; my home, my husband, friends, extended family (you know who you are), books and writing, the beauty and fragility and ferocity of nature.

Change is in front of me, and I reach out with both hands, eager. I step toward the challenge in spite of my doubts and fears. For if I do nothing different in my daily routine, I can create nothing different but the life I currently have. It is human nature to want more. It is also human nature to be unwilling to step outside the comfort of the familiar.

No one has ever made history by staying safe, by playing safe. It is only when we can see our comfort zone as a cage that we created that we can begin to expand our self-beliefs, expand our capabilities, take the next step and the next until we have forgotten what being inside our old comfort zone felt like. Then we will have truly begun to live.

May you begin your journey today. There is absolutely

no reason not to take one simple step toward your dreams and out of the cage you have made for yourself.

Consider this your sign.

I believe in you. I believe in me. I believe we can do this, whatever "this" means for you.

The above post was written when just the essence of this project had been whispered into my ear by Spirit (and a few dear friends).

See, the thing is, change is constantly happening. We can either resist it, go with it, or be the agent of change in our own lives. Which would you rather? Would you rather be in charge of the change in your life? Or would you rather be at the whim of change?

Of course, there are always things that come at us, willy-nilly, that we don't, and couldn't, expect. But everything else can be in our own hands, if we choose.

And why wouldn't you choose to be in charge of your own life? Ah. It's scary. Yeah, I get it. It is. But as I have said before, not doing something because you're scared is not a good reason. Especially for you, now, in your time of life.

You, right now, have the collective wisdom of your past and all that goes with it. You're a fount of knowledge. Things that scared you ten, twenty, or thirty years ago probably just make you chuckle now.

Why shouldn't you reach for your best life? Why shouldn't you go for that long-held, burning goal? Don't tell me you're too old. Or too young, for that matter. There are children all over the world being agents of change, starting businesses that help others, taking the adults at the United Nations to task, creating movements of change in many different countries. You can, too, if that's where your heart lies. Or you can travel the world. There's a myriad of things you can do, if you take the chance on yourself.

Your belief structure can change. Probably should change, if you have burning desires to reach a goal that you have let fall by the wayside. It's merely your belief structure, your perspective.

Life is sweet. Life is hard. The world is your friend. The world is full of strangers. My job is going to kill me. My job enables me to pay bills and plan for the future. Life itself is full of good and bad. How you react to life? That's on you and your belief structure.

If you see the world as inherently full of strangers, life inherently hard, and that your job is going to kill you, then that is what you will receive; strangers, more difficulties, and a job that causes your stress to go sky high, bringing with it all the health challenges that come with stress.

If you see the world as inherently full of friends, life inherently sweet, and your job as a way to keep yourself fed, clothed, and the lights on in your home, then you open yourself up to so many more blessings...such as a better job, better friends, and a happier future to come.

Am I simplifying life? *Of course* I am. But the truth remains. You see what you expect. You get what you expect. Only the truly unexpected will jolt your thinking, and even then, it may not change your belief structure simply because those beliefs of yours are set in stone. Or...are they?

You see, each of us chooses what to believe. We choose what to believe several times over, from when we are a child and on through our lives. WE CHOOSE WHAT WE BELIEVE. We choose who to listen to, and once a belief is set, not even factual evidence will shake our beliefs. Unless...we *choose* to change our belief.

Unfortunately, most of us choose what to believe without realizing that we're choosing. We choose it because our parents did, or our church tells us to, or our friends believe it and they're cool so we may as well believe it, too. We choose almost unconsciously.

Life is sweet. Life is hard. Knowing that we choose our own beliefs is a good first step. Knowing we can change our beliefs is another good step. We were given a mind, a heart, a body, and a soul for a reason, and to follow others blindly is not using the gifts we were given in a wise manner. It's past time to start analyzing our belief systems. Maybe there are some that need to be discarded, in favor of new beliefs. Think of it as mental spring cleaning.

Life is sweet. Life is hard. It is both and it is neither. It all depends on your belief structure.

September 20, 2018

Happy day, my lovelies! Every day brings new challenges, new joys, new sorrows. May today bring you what you need, in the amounts you need it, to help you navigate this life.

Strive to be kind, patient, and understanding, especially in situations where it would be just so easy to judge. So easy to let loose with a string of negatives.

In the end, all we have is each other. Hand clasping hand, arms around our shoulders, a loving touch when life gets hard.

Sending you a bundle of self-care. Oh, and long, luscious hugs. And love. Always.

14

DRAWING BOUNDARIES

Protect your creative or free time. Yes, even you who don't believe you're creative. You are.

Sometimes it feels impossible to draw that line and say "No." When pushed, we cave in and we agree to...whatever. But then we get stretched so thin, our entire being is watered down and our essence, our creativity and energy, is drained right out of us. We become sluggish, resentful, angry. We pick fights even though we're exhausted. To replenish that essence takes more time than we think we have, so frequently we ignore that desperate need for re-energizing, and instead throw ourselves furiously into more activity, thinking that will be the cure. A completed to-do list. More to focus on. Busy busy busy.

And we know this doesn't work, but we do it anyway.

Drawing boundaries is imperative. "No." is a complete sentence. Withdrawing from activities you've agreed to, when it suddenly feels too overwhelming, is absolutely okay. (I just had to do that, and it took all my nerve to send that message.)

But my time on this planet isn't for pleasing other

people or meeting other people's expectations. My time here is to meet or exceed MY expectations. To follow MY path and to cherish those I meet along the way.

Replenishing that which gets used up is also imperative. I take walks, read, snuggle with my hubby. Gaze into a campfire. Hug the pupdog. Stroke a purring kitty. Get soil under my fingernails because I'm planting in the garden. Go someplace I've never been, to do something I've never done. These are all a part of how I replenish and refill my creative well.

Whether you think yourself as a creative person or not, your store of patience and joy gets used up during your day/week. What delights you? What replenishes you, when you're worn thin from work or worry?

Keep a journal and if nothing else, start a daily gratitude practice. Maybe write down things that make you content, that keeps the sad at bay, as well as what you're grateful for. Just three things, each day, that you're grateful for. It can't hurt.

Your time here in this world is not for meeting or exceeding anyone's expectations but your own. Never forget that.

15

GRATITUDE

Oh, my loves. Don't look to others to complete you. Don't whine and complain when you have so much to be grateful for. Don't hide away from your wonderfulness. Above all, don't turn every moment of life into a competition where you must win, for you will, undoubtedly, lose when it counts the most.

Life is far too short. Celebrate yourself. Brush off negativity as often as you can. Seek inside you that which you most desire, for if you cannot find it there, it is not to be found.

Take the risk. Open your heart, your mind, your energies. Allow yourself to be overwhelmed, and then come to an understanding that embraces who you are. (That was me, at the Harvest Flames Autumn Meet in 2018 for the first time. Gods, I love those people at Phoenix Phyre.)

If you have a partner, value them. Listen to them. Be open to them. Cherish them, because life is fleeting. My life, right now, is the best it has ever been because...it is right now. I have wonderful memories, but those are in the past.

My present is damned near perfect. My future is in the future.

Breathe. Believe in the best of humankind. Take action when action is needed and frankly, it is needed more frequently than you may realize.

Often the best and brightest are drowned out by the loud and crude. Truth is lost amongst lies perpetuated by outside forces. Guard your truth. Know where you stand in these divisive times. Be willing, however, to see the person behind the rhetoric, especially if it is someone you know and/or love. Or maybe like.

Even wise men get fooled and cowed by bullies and naysayers. Be the voice of reason and truth, if you possibly can.

The world needs you.

When you're caught up in the whirlwind of stress, or success, or busy-ness, and your brain is fogged with details or worry or just on overload, give yourself a time out.

Take a few steps back, breathe deeply, and see with your rational mind. Whether it be huge success or huge disaster or just a cluster of little things that are driving you crazy, take a breath. Orient yourself. What is your goal? What are you aiming for right now?

It is easy to get diverted away from our purpose. Check in with yourself, and those you trust, and listen to your instincts.

My family is not perfect; neither is my life. I choose to focus on the positive, because I hope to bring more positivity into my world. Because, you know, there are good things right on the horizon that are coming closer to me, every day that I decide it is so. There are good things on the horizon for you, too.

We can all do amazing things, if we decide it is so.

I mention this because I don't want anyone thinking that I'm superior. I'm not, nor do I think of myself as better than you. The only person I'm trying to be better than is the person I was yesterday. Writing this book has made me squirmy, hence the disclaimer.

Now more than ever, I know how small I am in this vast ocean of people and words and love and hate and anger and joy. If I can make a ripple in that ocean, a ripple of love, then I'll have done something to be proud of.

Won't you join me? The world needs our ripples of love. Ripples of joy, tenderness, compassion. We can do it, one person at a time. Ready?

"We ought to do good to others as simply and naturally as a horse runs, or a bee makes honey, or a vine bears grapes season after season without thinking of the grapes it has borne."
Marcus Aurelius Antoninus

Today, do three things, just for you, that lift your spirit. Find gratitude for three things in your life. And reach out to three people you've been meaning to talk to.

Walk lightly on the earth, breathe deep, find a moment

to be still within yourself. The world will not collapse if you are unavailable for a bit.

Dream. Dream big. Act on your dreams. Keep a positive spirit and ignore those who would downsize your dreams.

Don't let anyone tell you that you aren't worthy, not even that snarky little voice inside your head. Because you are.

16

ON LOVE

Love is the greatest force on this planet. It is stronger than hate, it overcomes fear, it thrives even when given no encouragement. Loving other people can be one of the most radical acts you do.

Giving your respectful time and attention to those who are not like you, who don't live or worship or dress like you, is important. It can even be seen as an act of love for the human race. We are all one race. We have but one planet. As the current saying goes, there is no Planet B.

Love humanity. Love our planet. Spread the love. Be radical in your love, and never be ashamed. Never regret loving, no matter the outcome. Stand against those who would divide us, those who would plunder our planet for a few to get wealthier. Love fiercely, love joyfully, love radically.

April 29, 2016

It's Friday, lovelies. Know that you are beautiful, just as you are, and that no one way of eating, no self-help book, no exercise or clutter-free plan, and no soul mate will make you happy if you're not already soul-deep in love with yourself.

Those people who proclaim they know the "one true way" to live, well... give them the side-eye, and pass on by. They don't know your soul. They can't make the best decisions for you, so don't invest in what they're selling.

As always, if you need a hug, or some love, stop by my house, virtual or otherwise. I'm almost always around. xoxo...and here's to you, my lovely.

I know that several times in this book I mention how you need to love yourself before you can love others. What I have neglected to mention until now is that there may very well come a time when someone loves you before YOU love you, and you are honestly baffled.

They're a great person! They have their act together! They live like a grown-up. How can they love me? You might say. (Or maybe that's just the romance writer in me.)

If you care for them at all, if their love warms you from the inside out, then take it and use it to look at yourself through their eyes. You just might find yourself flowering into the person they see, the person you have been all along. You just might find yourself learning and growing in love.

Isn't that a wonderful thing?

This is true of friendships, too, by the way, not just romantic relationships. My friends have helped me see me through their eyes, and while it can be embarrassing, it's also enlightening.

17

ON GIVING BIRTH

We are all connected. I know this. I experienced this. The first time it happened, I was in labor with my oldest son.

I felt the whispers of connection while I was in the shower, shaving my legs, running the razor over my skin between contractions, which were still several minutes apart. (Am I the only about-to-give-birth woman who didn't want my obstetrician to see my hairy legs? I don't think so...)

That sense, that rhythm of life. The ebb and flow, planet wide, of birth, life, death, rippled through me. Source of all.

The connection came through stronger when I was close to giving birth. At the hospital, as a contraction gripped me, I felt the pulsing of a million heartbeats in time with my own, all of them working with me to bring this life into the world. As if the entire planet turned toward me and gave me strength.

I could hear the waves crash to the shores on beaches across the planet. I felt the forests breathing with me, felt that ebb and flow of my pain shared with every other laboring woman in the world, and I have never felt so connected in my life. I felt the passing of other souls, even as I gave a last push and my son was born.

I've only told this to one, maybe two other people. This is the first time I've tried to put that feeling into words on paper, and I don't think I quite captured it.

My takeaway was, we are all connected, to Source and to each other. What we do here in the United States affects those in a small country on the other side of the planet. We either strengthen each other and our world, or we tear it down.

I felt those heartbeats in my chest. I breathed to the rhythm of the waves, the rhythm of the trees.

How anyone can believe that each of us doesn't have any effect on the planet is totally beyond my comprehension.

The same is true with birthing a book, a program, a piece of art, a business. Any time you create something that hadn't previously existed, you're connected to the world. To Source.

The Universe, Source, wants your creation. Source will give you what you need to create; you just have to do the work.

18

ON LOSS AND DEATH, WILLS AND ESTATE PLANNING

Sometimes it takes a while to see the need for thinking ahead. 2017 was my year of grief; 2018 became my year of healing. A part of that healing was to look to the future, in much the same way my parents had, so many years ago. No book about seizing life with both hands should ignore death, which is why I included the following.

October 5, 2018

The death of a loved one is like an earthquake. One hard jolt, seemingly lasting forever, and...they are gone.

Then come the aftershocks—the memories, a resemblance you see in someone in a car passing you, or on the street—the curve of a cheek, hair color, a song. A favorite movie, or a flower. A scent on the air, or a taste. You don't know when the aftershocks will hit, or how often.

They cluster, rattle you until you're not sure if the ground is shaking under you or not, your heart aches, and then...nothing, for days. Weeks. Months. You can think of your loved one without so much pain. It can even make you smile, at times. You think you're "over it".

Boom, another cluster pops up, shaking you again with memories, with tears. As time passes, these aftershocks will eventually hold memories you greet with fondness and love, and the memories don't quite hurt as much as they did in the beginning, but it still hurts. Oh yes, it hurts.

That death is never forgotten. Nor do we necessarily get better at riding out the aftershocks.

It sucks, but that's life. The upside is having the joy of loving so deeply, which causes us to feel the loss so deeply.

September 25, 2018

To the brokenhearted...to the lost. To those who don't know where they will sleep tonight. To those who have bills they don't know how they will pay. To the ones who feel they have nowhere to turn, and nothing left to live for. To those who have lost loved ones and whose hearts are aching with emptiness.

To those who lie sleepless, worrying that you've just completely fucked up your entire life, and you don't know how to explain it to your spouse/boss/best friend.

I care.

I can't provide you with a home, or a purpose, or money to pay your bills...but I care. I send out love to the Universe for you. I send out positivity to the Universe for you, that the answers will appear. I send out hugs to the Universe for you, so that you will know loving arms.

Many people will think what I do is negligible. Airy fairy. Stupid.

It is all I know how to do at this point, for a world that is hurting. When I have more, I will do more. Until then, I do what I can.

When my father died in March 2017, I lost it. My brother Greg and my husband kept me together.

Dad's family trust planning (note: family trusts are not just for wealthy people) saved us a lot of grief. My brother Greg and I drove together down to San Diego many, many times between March and August after Dad died, first for the wake/memorial we had at the house, and then for all the stuff we needed to do regarding his estate. This time together bonded us more than ever. He's my rock. He's my big brother. I love him to pieces and I always will.

We spent several weekends clearing out Dad's house, once we were at that point and had a Realtor. Fifteen boxes of books that were just copies of the ones he wrote. Then another twenty or so boxes of books in his library. All were donated to the San Carlos Library, who were happy to have them. Once his house was sold and escrow closed, we had no reason to go back. The end of an era.

My parents moved into that house on October 6, 1959, before the electricity was even turned on. It was the house I came home to after I was born. The one place I had felt the safest all through my childhood. I know how lucky I am. I do. Selling the house was the right thing to do but oh, how much did it hurt when we realized the buyer lied to us and was a flipper, rather than someone who would live in it and love it as much as we did? A lot. It hurt me a lot.

Aside from the house, it took almost a year to close out Dad's estate, but luckily, we didn't have to go through probate due to his planning ahead. A few items in his will (and addenda to the Trust) saddened us, even though we knew about it ahead of time. He was always careful to give us updates on what he was planning.

It was his money, not ours. Greg and I both agreed that whatever he chose to do with it was fine with us. We may not have agreed with Dad's decisions, but again – not our money.

Tom and I had written wills just before we went to Europe for the first time after 9/11, in 2003 or 2004. Just in case. Our sons were young, and if the unthinkable happened again, we wanted them to be cared for. We let those wills stand for another decade plus.

But almost 18 months after my daddy died, we finally got down to business and hired a lawyer we knew to do our trust/estate planning, our wills, our power of attorney and power of health care. Our sons weren't children anymore, they didn't need guardians. But Tom and I did, just in case. We did DNRs with conditions. It took time, it took some difficult thought (after all, no one LIKES to plan for their death), but eventually, after spending an hour getting pages and pages notarized at AAA (free, because it's a perk of membership), it was done. We funded the trust with our home. We're ready for anything at this point, though our children may not be.

Plan for your death, because that is the one certainty we all share but rarely talk about. If we are born, we shall die. That is the circle, the cycle of life.

Tonight's writings took me back to the days of my daddy's passing. My heart and soul are still sore. What I share in this book is both my heart and my soul.

Life is laughter. Life is love. Life is pain. Life is sorrow. Life is passion. Life is regret. Life is joy. Life is every emotion you can imagine, and again and again and again, unceasing.

Relentless. Life demands us to feel. Life demands us to respect. Life demands us to know who we are.

Like the waves of the ocean. The ocean is the wave, and the wave is the ocean. We are life, and life is us.

Grief comes upon us in a wave and recedes at its will.

If we numb ourselves to life, are we truly alive? If we close ourselves off to the joys and the sorrows of life, can it be said that we still live?

Exist. Yes, maybe we exist when we cut ourselves off from the world.

But live? I don't think so.

Both my parents died in the hospital. Both of my paternal grandparents died at home. In September of 1986, grandpa had just come in to have lunch after cleaning out the gutters of his house. Grandma Hazel was putting his sandwich together; the phone rang. She turned to answer it. When she turned back less than a minute later, Grandpa Merle had died, his head pillowed on his arms, draped on the table.

Grandma Hazel died on Valentine's day in 1991. My Uncle Kenny called my dad; she'd died in her sleep, in the comfort of her own bed.

My father was alone when he died; I had to go back to work the day before. My mother? I didn't even know she was in the hospital, as my dad didn't want to worry me. He'd stepped out of her room for a moment, and only the caregiver was there with her when she passed away, so at least she wasn't alone.

My brother Scott died at home, with my mother holding his hand.

My family history is why the below post was written.

July 14, 2018

On the drive home from work a few days ago, I came to the realization that I wasn't afraid of death. I don't think I've ever been afraid of it. What I fear, instead, is the process leading up to death...possible pain, hospitalization, loss of dignity, loss of personality, and being alone. If I have my way, I'll go peacefully in my sleep, having gone to bed the night before like every other night of my life.

But as I've been writing this, I have come to a realization...the process leading up to death is, quite simply, the act of living. So instead of fearing the possibilities of how I might die, I shall simply live, and love, and enjoy the hell out of the time I have here on this planet with the people I love. Whether that ends up being thirty years, or much less, doesn't matter. What will matter is how I live, and not, in the slightest, how I die.

I say this, knowing how my brother Scott died. In 1990, he'd been diagnosed with AIDS. He had been home with my parents, in a hospice situation (in what had been my bedroom), since January of 1993. On that night in March of 1993, he had fallen into a coma, and when my parents realized that the next morning, my mother held his hand while sitting in her wheelchair at his bedside until he died, early that afternoon.

In 2007, my mother died after being in the hospital for six days (and my brother and I weren't informed), with a woman who I hope was caring enough to hold her hand by her side when Dad had to take a break (but...issues...she was mom's caregiver and, later, my dad's caregiver, and... yeah, lots of issues here).

My father died in March of 2017 in a rehabilitation hospital, after breaking some small bones in his back during a fall six weeks earlier. The breaks had gone undiagnosed for over a month, and he was in so much pain until finally he was admitted to the hospital and had the proper imagery done. He was moved to a rehabilitation hospital, but it soon became apparent that he would never be able to do the exercises they wanted him to do, and he would need to be moved to a different type of hospital.

Two days before he died, after listening to someone only he could hear, he talked to me about us having to leave. He tried to get out of bed, but I pulled the covers over him and tucked him in. I told him that it was a journey I couldn't go on as yet, that he'd have to go alone.

He nodded, then talked about a man smoking a pipe sitting on the clock near the ceiling. Out of the blue, he started singing *Home, Home on the Range* so I joined in and sang with him. I held his hand, gnarled with arthritis and so very dear to me. When he said he was going to rest a bit, I kissed him, pressed my cheek to his, and breathed him in before saying goodbye. Before telling him I loved him, very much.

Luckily, he knew me right up to the end. I wish I could have been there when he died, but my guess is he would have waited until I had left his side for some reason or another. He died two days after the last time I saw him, and just one day after I'd worked with the rehabilitation hospital to move him home for hospice.

Losing him ripped the heart out of my chest, because I was always a daddy's girl. The love my husband and brother and friends showed me put my heart back into its place, but there's still a daddy-shaped hole there that no one will ever fill.

19

OUR CHAOTIC, ANGRY WORLD

Our Chaotic, Angry World
You all know where we are now. Often, when I have all these feelings bottled up inside me regarding our world today, the only place I can put them is on Facebook. Strange, I know. But it has been a healing move for me, and hopefully others.

September 27, 2017

We are all made of star stuff. We all bleed red when we are cut. We all love, laugh, cry, grieve. Please, my friends. Don't let a tweet from a mean-spirited person distract you from the fact that we are stronger together.

I don't know, anymore, how to handle divisive, bitter people without becoming divisive and bitter, too. I've finally realized that I don't have to 'handle' those divisive, bitter people. It's not my job to change other people's minds. It's not my job to educate.

It is my job, however, to dig deep into issues that bother me, to see the whole picture, and not just one side. It is my job to empathize. It is my job to help out when I can, with whatever I can. And it is my job to love fiercely, live my truth, speak my truth to those who may have ears to hear.

I won't play ostrich, though I am comfortable doing so. Neither will I puff up with outrage over what's happening in the world, because frankly, I'd be outraged all the time, and that gets exhausting.

September 7, 2017

Changes. The world is roiling with them right now, from the fires and the floods and the hurricanes, to the wars across the planet.

It's time we all took our Judgy-McJudgerson horse-blinders off, and put on our kind, compassionate, and intelligent glasses.

Reach out when you can. Ask for help if you need it. Give freely that which you can give and accept that which comes your way. Energy feeds energy, whether that be from love, or from hate.

Choose love.

We're in a time of transition. United, we stand. How do you want to be remembered?

20

I CAN'T DO IT ANYMORE

August 22, 2018

I can't do it. I've tried. I've tried to live in a place of hate and anger at the "other side," I've tried to be righteous in that anger. But you know what? That's not how I'm made.

I'm made *of* love, *to* love. I'm a sunny side of the street person. I am laughter and joy and holding hands and hugging strangers. I am a firm believer that there is good in this world, and that love will prevail.

Hating hurts. And when I see the haters out there, those who have to put others down in order to feel their own worth, I feel sorry for them. I know they are hurting; I know they are in pain, and that's why they do what they do (in part, at any rate). And I wish I could help them.

But if I've learned anything over my lifetime, it's that love and happiness starts with ourselves. If we cannot love ourselves, how can we truly love others? If we cannot find happiness within ourselves, how can we share that with others? For happiness, and love, start from within.

I learned a few very profound things this past weekend. But the one that struck me the most is this.

"Your life is not about you. It's about the lives of everyone you touch."
– Lisa Nichols

Your touch can be a loving one, or it can be a hateful, hurting one. Lisa also said, "No one was put here to keep silent." So, I'm not keeping silent. I'm speaking up, and saying I will not apologize for my love, or for my light, or for seeing the best in people, as best I can. (I mean, come on. Everyone has a snarky side.)

Being angry and hateful causes internal pain, as well as external pain. I can't live there, I just can't. And I so hope that you can't live there, either.

This is why I write about love. The world will tear itself apart if we let fear, hate, and anger rule us. Love mends. Love heals. Love starts with you.

Because frankly? Sometimes we suck at believing in ourselves, much less in each other. We are all more than we think we are. We are more loving, more daring, more intelligent. We are more flexible mentally. We are more capable than we dream. We are stronger, wiser, and full of poetry and beauty, but we need to believe we are.

Never stop learning, never think there is only one way to do something. Never stop believing in the good of humanity, even though that gets difficult at times. Never stop knowing that beauty runs through your soul and spreads through you to the rest of the world. There is only one YOU. You deserve the best of yourself. It always goes back to... Whether you think you can, or think you can't, you're right.

June 20, 2018

My loves...not all of my life can be sunshine and rainbows, so my feed can't be all sunshine and rainbows. If I lose readers or friends because of my beliefs, so be it.

My heart is heavy. My country is going through some dark times, and for the first time in my life I doubt our governmental system of checks and balances. I doubt the abilities of our elected officials to rein in the creature who holds the office of the Presidency. I even doubt that we'll have another Presidential election in 2020 that won't be a farce. And my doubts have me scared to my bones.

These are dangerous times. I wish civil discourse hadn't died. I wish science and intelligence hadn't been so thoroughly dismissed (and in certain areas of the country, that's always been the case from what I understand). I wish our government hadn't gotten so thoroughly derailed. I wish that the integrity of all news sources hadn't been tainted by a few, owned by men with a fiendish agenda. I wish...so many things.

Not to go backward, no. Because the past wasn't any better; with regard to the bigotry and hatred of those who were "different," that has been a way of life here in the United States since the first white men set foot on the land and systematically stole it from the Native Americans.

But to go forward, to tear down the bigotry of the past and create something new and better, will take the grit, the humility, the determination, and all the love inside each of us to forge a new United States of America, one where superiority/inferiority is no longer conferred due merely to the color of our skin or the amount of our bank balance. Where it isn't an issue at all, no matter what.

It's a pipe dream, some will say, and maybe so. I'm delusional, some will say. Maybe so. I'm an idiot special snowflake stupid liberal old white chick who should shut up and sit down. Well, that ain't gonna happen, boyo.

I'm willing to dream that pipe dream of mine, and work for it. Call me names if it makes you feel better. I'm trying my best to love you anyway. (Though I'd really appreciate it if you didn't make it so. damn. hard. to love you. And this is the Universal 'you', by the way.)

My wish for you is to find peace in the small things, do what you can for the greater good, so that at night, when you meet your own gaze in the mirror, you can feel good about yourself.

21

SELF-CARE

This is a post from 2015. I remember waking up and needing to write this down, so I did. I believe it was in response to many other posts the day before on Facebook, where people were just...wallowing.

The Don'ts Take Care of Me

Don't play the music that makes you sad if you don't want to be sad.

Don't worry about what you can't control (such as other people's actions).

Don't take the world's problems onto your shoulders.

Don't take your friends' problems onto your shoulders.

Don't look for validation anywhere else but from within yourself.

Don't lower your expectations. If others don't measure up, that's on them, not you.

Don't let go of your dreams. Despite whatever odds, if you hold true, they may come to pass. If you don't hold onto your dreams, they can't come to pass.

Don't hang around waiting to be noticed. Because who has time for that?

Don't take things personally. Most of the time, whatever it is has nothing to do with you.

Don't always be the one to reach out first.

Don't ever give up, if it's something you truly want.

And the hardest one...

Don't close your heart, for you never know where love will find you.

Self-care is important. It's real, and it's necessary. Whether you're male or female, non-binary, or other identifying, you need to take care of yourself so you can care for others.

Americans aren't good at self-care. We don't take enough vacations. We work through our lunches. We're paranoid that if we take a sick day, we'll get fired. I get it, I do. I've worked in corporate settings for over 20 years, and for a long time I felt the same way.

Intellectually, I knew I needed to take care of myself, but sometimes my work ethic (well, that's what I like to call it) got in the way and I'd go to work sick. As I've gotten older, I've taken more sick days when I've been sick, I've gone to more doctor appointments, and now I make no apology for my actions.

It was brought home to me this year how important it is to stay home when you're ill. I'd gone to work and for two days in a row, my right eye was bugging me. As I have Dry Eye Syndrome, I just thought it was that, but by the end of the second day, I kind of figured it was something else. I mentioned to my boss and a couple of my coworkers that I couldn't see well out of my right eye, it was bothering me, and I apologized.

I went to the eye doctor the next morning, and lo and

behold, I had pink eye. A very mild case of it, and only in one eye. When I told my eye doc that my boss was immunocompromised, he told me to take the rest of the week off, as 24 hours was usually okay when medicated but 48 hours was better (this was on a Wednesday).

When I got home, meds in hand, I emailed everyone at the office, told them what I had, and told them I'd see them the following Monday.

Well.

When I got to the office on Monday, my boss had pink eye. HE CAME INTO THE OFFICE WITH PINK EYE. Ahem. Not only that, but he had it about fifty times worse than I had (compromised immune system, remember). What took me six days to completely clear up took him a couple of months and a few different medications.

Self-care is important. It's not just about you, boo. It's also about the people around you. If I had realized what I had and gone to the eye doc the first day, would my boss have been infected?

Probably, as pink eye can be transmitted via paper, and we were handing papers back and forth all day long. But still. This is just a simple episode of pink eye that turned dire for my boss.

Later that year, I had an upper respiratory infection. I stayed home an entire week (and it took me 4 medications and 10 weeks to fully recover). If I had gone in that first week, and if my boss had caught my infection, he could have died.

Think when you're sick. Think! Trust me, the world will keep turning if you don't go to work that day.

Of course, self-care doesn't just include physical ailments.

Wear the Pearls

The most important piece of self-care that I gave myself for mental reasons happened in the summer of 1993. My brother Scott had died in March of that year, when I was three months' pregnant with my second son. I was working for a large privately-held computer software company at the time called Candle Corporation (long since absorbed by IBM).

By July of 1993, I was in a bit of physical pregnancy distress, as in everything hurt. Not to mention it seemed like I saw Scott around every corner and in every car going the other way on the freeway.

I took the morning off and went to a pregnancy massage therapist, thinking to work the kinks out of my back. I know now that I was severely stressed (though I didn't think so then), and she must have seen it in me.

She started asking questions about my life, whether I was happy with my pregnancy, how I was doing, what was going on in my life at the time. All before she started the massage.

When I told her about my brother, I started crying. And then she said ... if you don't handle your grief, your baby will be born sad and deformed.

I was horrified. I got up off the table and left without paying and without the massage. Instead of going to work like a good worker bee, I drove the length of the San Fernando Valley, up and over the mountains, to Free Zuma Beach (called such because you don't have to pay to park. Regular Zuma Beach is one driveway over).

I sat on the beach and cried. Talked to Scott. Asked the gods to give me a happy baby, untouched by my pain. Put my feet in the water and washed my hands in it.

This was before cell phones. My husband didn't know where I was. Luckily, no one called home looking for me, I guess because I had a "doctor's appointment" and I was pregnant.

I needed that mental health day. I needed the time beside the waves, the salt, the cool Pacific Ocean on my slightly swollen feet. I needed the time to be alone with the pain of losing my brother, as well as time to reassure the little one inside me that he was just fine. Happy, loving, and a whole person. And yes, my youngest son is a happy, loving, and whole person.

My point is, sometimes you need to go off-grid. Sometimes you need to grieve or regroup. Or maybe just... have a spa day, even if you're doing your own nails. You know what? The world won't end. Your workplace won't blow up. You'll still have a job the next day.

Hell, you might even get flowers from your boss the next day (which I did).

22

THE IMPORTANCE OF SCENT

The scent of the ocean brings me memories such as the above. Other scents bring other memories.

It's funny how they can carry such meaning and can send our emotions into a tizzy (either up or down). One morning we dropped by Lowes to pick up work gloves for me, and to see if any plants needed to come home with us. Normally, I stay within the annuals section, as planting bigger things like trees or flowering bushes aren't my thing (because our soil sucks here). Somehow, I found myself in front of the gardenia plants, and had to lean in and enjoy the fragrance.

As I did, memories tumbled through me, sent tears to my eyes. Gardenias were my mother's most favorite flower. She carried them in her wedding bouquet; I wore gardenias in my hair at my wedding. She kept planting gardenia bushes, but they never grew lush like our next-door neighbor's bush did. And it hit me that she was gone, that this time of year that she loved would pass without her. My memories of Christmas and Mom are entwined, and it struck my heart so hard.

Now, Mom passed away in 2007, and this happened several years later; so, this wasn't my first Christmas without her. But there in the garden section I had to wipe my eyes, collect myself. Being seen crying in front of the gardenias would just lead to headaches and explanations and I didn't want to have/do either of those things. When the hubs came by, my eyes were dry and I went to pick up my gloves from where I'd left them as he got in line. A few more tears were shed, and quickly wiped away, before I could join him and continue our morning.

It was a reminder to both the child in me and the writer in me that scents are primal, etched into our brain along with the emotion evoked; they are necessary in writing, and unavoidable in life.

August 3, 2018

It's been a weird night/day. I woke up about 2:30am, as I usually do. Sipped water, rolled over, and instead of drifting back into sleep, my brain began to sing...I think it was "Something's Coming" from West Side Story. Anyway.

Once my brain starts singing, it's difficult to get back to sleep. Instead, my brain then trotted out everything I have to do. I mean, everything. From bills that needed to get paid, to boxes that need sorting out, to a question about a couple insurance bills. Oh and damn it, I owe my brother an edit. And will my paycheck cover everything plus, with extra for gas?

I took a bath, thinking that would ease me back into sleep mode.

As I kind of dozed in the tub, I thought it had worked. Got out, went back to bed, started to drift...then

"Somewhere" started playing in my brain (also from West Side Story), and all the other to-dos from earlier came flooding back. Then it was the writing...how I'm not writing tight enough, fast enough. How there's no way I can possibly finish this book per the deadline I set in order to get it to my editor. Oh, and now I need a launch plan, because the Caine series is coming out again with new material, new covers, and new pricing, so more work needed to get done...

By now, it's after four in the morning and I'm exhausted and my head is pounding. I mean, rip-my-skull-off pounding. I leave my comfy bed and my snuggly man and go out into the living room, plop down on the couch, and I think I cried a bit which only made my head worse.

And then my mom's grandfather clock chimed the half hour...and I dropped into sleep. A light one, but still. When it chimed the three-quarters hour, I dropped a bit deeper. By the time five AM rang, I was out. (It was my parents, giving me their love.)

The cat came and went. When Tom finally woke me at whatever time, my head still hurt, just not as ferociously...but the weight of everything I "had" to do hadn't gone away, so I slept some more. And then some more.

Ultimately, I didn't go into work. I felt fragile and my head hurt. But after some green juice, and a good breakfast, I got my planner out and my washi tape and my stickers and my pens, because damn it, if I had to make to-do lists, I was going to enjoy myself.

Some of my anxiety was alleviated, just by writing it all down. Then I paid bills. I found a solution to the writing issue - find this certain lesson in a class I'm taking, read it over again, then go over my work to make sure it's as tight as

I can make it before I continue on. I found the lesson but didn't take the next step because fragile.

But I remembered I had a release and did some quick marketing on it (add to list). Then...I napped. And in the afternoon, my lovely husband and I went to see Christopher Robin.

In a way, I felt like I was Christopher...working hard for woozles (in this case, each woozle was an item on my to-do list in the middle of the night) but with no end in sight. No joy. And when Christopher Robin finally realizes what's important, I remembered, too (well, okay, I remembered a LOT earlier because there's a lot of aw... moments with Pooh, sniff...).

To make a long story short (too late!), I crossed off some items on my to-do list, and the others will get done in due time. I stopped being prey to my to-do list and started living for, well, myself and those I love. Why give my attention to that which ramps up my anxiety? Why not just shift that to the side, and be good to myself? Everything will get done in due time.

May your woozles be easily beaten back, and may you remember that this is life, right now, right in front of you. And oh...sometimes doing nothing leads to the most marvelous something, indeed.

23

CREATIVITY IS FOR EVERYONE

I have known many engineers. Many geologists. Many software gurus. And all of them didn't consider what they did as creative.

Are you fucking kidding me? How scientists of all kinds don't often see their work as creative stuns me. Their professions came about because someone had a brain fart about rocks, or about zeroes and ones, or about space, water, our lungs, etc.

Sometimes I think scientists are the most creative people of all the people on the planet. They just have a discipline of the mind, a deep curiosity, and the focus and desire for answers not easily found that most of us don't have.

I am a writer and a doodler and every now and then, I paint. I used to be a ballet dancer, then a musical theater dancer. Now I dance in my living room when no one is watching.

In my mind, everyone is a creative, whether they believe it to be true or not.

Everyone. What would you do, if no one was watching,

criticizing your effort, judging you at each step? Maybe go do that. Give it a try.

September 6, 2018

Some novels just gush out. They pour from brain to fingers to the screen in a satisfying swarm of words that all seem to make sense. Words that have direction and life and vivacity and yes, the story will need editing, but the core is there.

Other novels start that way, then they slog. Writing them is like pulling teeth. The first couple chapters get rewritten and rewritten and rewritten until it "feels" right, and then the floodgates open once more.

And others are start and stop. Start and stop. A hundred words here. Two hundred there. Ten, fifteen minutes of time snatched from your life, instead of a long, luxurious swathe of hours to get the words down.

I have to remind myself to breathe during the start and stop times. That forward momentum is forward momentum. Two hundred words every day is better than no words every day.

Creativity takes time, patience, persistence. Whether you're writing, or painting, designing jewelry, or coming up with the theory of relativity, figuring out how to get clean water to a desert area, or throwing pots...being creative takes mental energy that can easily get depleted from the other stuff we have to do in our lives, leaving nothing left over.

But if you're meant to do the thing, then you'll find a way to do the thing. Trust in that.

An underlying, unspoken thread recently for me has been, believe in yourself. As I stand trembling on the edge of professional change, I have that thought in a mental death grip.

I believe in myself, damn it.

Another unspoken thread was to be open to learning new ways of doing things. There is no surer way to mediocrity, in my opinion, than believing you know everything there is to know about your profession. Even when the tools of change are put into your hands, if you believe you're at the top of your game and there is no more to learn? Then you will drop those newer tools handed to you as insignificant against your own knowledge. And you will lose because of it.

Stay open to learning new tools, new ways of thinking, new ways of doing, even if you've been in your business for ten, twenty, thirty years or more. Things change, and that is the only constant. Technology changes. To not keep up with technology, at the very least, is to be willing to not be heard, in my opinion. Your opinion may vary, of course.

I have believed, for over four decades now, that the day I stop learning is the day I die. At the rate I'm going, I'm going to live forever.

Believe. Learn. Grow. Stay open to the wonders of the world. Sending love and hugs, always.

Breathe today. Know that you're right where you should be for now, and nothing is stopping you from moving ahead to wherever you desire to be.

You. Are. Enough. Just as you are. Your light shines brightly when you forget to be cautious, when you forget to be afraid, and just allow yourself to be. Shine, so others can see your light. Shine, so others may find hope.

There are no guarantees for the future. So do the work, enjoy the play time. Make the phone call you've been putting off. Kiss, make love, hold hands, hug, get physical. Move your body. Plant a seed. Clear away the detritus in the garden. Observe the world around you through the eyes of the innocent, rather than the jaded person you may have become.

Everything is in reach. The Universe is on your side. Now, all you have to do is ask.

Do the work, so when opportunity knocks, you are ready, willing, and able to step through that door and into a new stage in this life.

All you have to do is the work. That's it.

Wait. What?

Ah, yes. Nothing is free. Most of us aren't born with wealth behind us. Most of us are lucky if our parents can pay the bills.

You need to do the work to get ahead. That doesn't mean going into burnout mode, though. It just means that, whatever you wish to do and excel at, learn that. Learn it as though it meant your life, because you know what? That passion of yours just might make a difference between reaching that goal you so desire and not.

If you're not willing to work for the reward that you desire, what does motivate you?

24

LIFE'S A PUZZLE

Have you seen that meme about how you buy a book from Ikea, and what you get is a box full of nothing but individual letters? Consonants and vowels and commas and periods all jumbled up together, and all you have to do is put them together in the right order, and you have your book?

Authors love that one, because frequently that's what writing a book is like. As well, frequently people we know will say, oh yeah, I've got a book I'm going to write.

Um. Moving on.

Life, I think, is more like a puzzle. I've been playing this puzzle game on my phone lately, and the game gives you a choice of how many pieces you use. Twenty-four is the smallest number of pieces, and 630 is the highest number. I usually play with 280 pieces, the second to highest number. I also keep rotate off, so however the piece is shown me is the proper orientation. I suppose that's cheating...eh, I'm okay with that.

I choose to not have the background shadowed with the photo that I'm puzzling, so often I lose track of the whole picture. It's the oddest thing. Individual pieces catch my attention, and I'm certain I'm looking at pieces belonging to a shimmering lake, when in reality it's a rain-splashed asphalt road. Or I could swear it's a sunset, when it's actually the sun reflected on the ocean.

The more I play, the faster my eye gets at recognizing shape and color and what pieces should go where.

Pattern recognition. Humans are wired for it, so much so that when we see something that we cannot immediately understand, our brain fills in the gaps. Sometimes, it fills in the gaps with wrong information. That right there is why often witnesses in court cases are not reliable...our brains fill in the gaps with the information it *thinks* it sees but is not true.

The same goes with all those trick word games you see on social media. You know, like...

Fi uoy nac daer siht, uoy era a suineg.

The fact is, our brains insert missing letters, unscramble words, add in missing words, and in general get us the information we need to understand the message. Our brains also fill in pictures that aren't complete. Which is often where the witness fails to be accurate. Not our fault...it's our brain that's in charge.

However, the more we do puzzles of all kinds, the more flexible our brains become, and the more able we are to see the pattern in everything.

Sometimes, the puzzle is easy. For instance, once I accidentally hit the "24" pieces button, and the entire puzzle was shown on my phone screen. I could see, at a glance, where almost everything went just because I could see all the pieces, AND the size of the puzzle.

When I'm working with 280 pieces, the screen on my phone shows only one-sixth of the puzzle. (Following the timeless advice of my brother Greg, I always do the edge pieces first.) Not having the picture to go by is, for me, a lot of fun.

I love my puzzle app. It keeps my brain sharp.

In real life, often the puzzle of our life has missing pieces. Or we turn and turn and turn a piece, only to realize it doesn't go where we thought it should. It might not even be a piece of our life puzzle; instead, it's a piece of some other person's life puzzle...but it takes time for us to understand that.

In real life, sometimes someone sweeps our life puzzle pieces into the trash, and all we're left with is the one piece that is us.

You know what? That's the only piece you need. You can build yourself up, create a new puzzle, and fit into that new life.

Oh, I'm not gonna lie and tell you it's easy. I expect it isn't easy to rebuild from scratch. I don't know personally, as I've never had to give up everything and rebuild, but I know people who have.

Okay, I know characters in books who have, and that's practically the same thing. You know why? Because that's often how I learn about the human condition. I read. I read a lot. I read romance, mysteries, science fiction, personal growth, biographies, philosophy, psychology...thrillers...the daily newspaper...I read a lot.

I've had to rebuild my sense of self, however, more than once. For instance, in 1980 I was stranded at a hotel in Great Falls, Montana, with fifty-plus other people without our last paycheck because the tour manager of our bus & truck company of L'il Abner was arrested for writing bad checks across five states. I ended up walking out of the hotel through a side door with my luggage, and not paying the bill that the tour company was supposed to pay. That did, definitely, change my sense of self.

When I became a mom for the first time (1990). And the second time (1993). My self-image needed to include these babies that I adored, which took some time.

When I became a manager (2006). I was better at it than the first time I had some managerial control (1999-2001 – yeah, I really sucked at it.).

When I had surgery for the acoustic neuroma (2010). It took me three solid years to get back on track, mentally.

When I got my first novel contract (2010). When I got my second novel contract (2014). When I spoke at my first pagan gathering (2018). All three of these moments expanded my sense of self, expanded my knowledge of who I could become.

And now. I'm rebuilding who I am, and what I stand for, and what I will, and will not, talk about publicly. Or maybe I should say, I'm expanding who I am, publicly.

I think we rebuild ourselves many times in our lives without being consciously aware of it.

All you need is that puzzle piece that is you. You're the key. You're the one who completes the picture.

Does any of this make sense? I hope so. It made sense in my brain before I started writing it down. I actually had finished my work for the day and was puzzling, which then got my brain to working, and which then pushed me back to the keyboard.

Rebuilding may not be easy, but in the long run I believe it is worthwhile.

Just do your best to not hand over pieces of your puzzle to other people who won't cherish them, and slot them in place for you when the time is right. You deserve the good, always.

Oh man. After writing this and letting it sit for a day, now I'm all conflicted. Have I given puzzles for my boys to put together? Have I been a good parent? (I hope so. They haven't fled the nest, so I believe I haven't totally fucked them up.) Will I be a good grandparent if they ever have kids?

Everyone has self-doubt. That should be the first thing and the last thing written in that parental manual that comes with every baby born. Oh wait...

Doubting yourself is normal. When doubt squeezes your positivity out of your head, allow it. Go ahead and doubt as hard as you can for five minutes. Then kick that doubt to the curb and keep on blazing your own path.

You're the only you this world has. The world needs your best self. *You* need your best self. Yes, we have ups and downs, but overall, I guarantee, you at your best will win out more often than not, if that's where you focus your attention.

25

WINDING DOWN

The morning still holds that early hush. Traffic is a low rumble in the distance, and the sky is that very pale white-blue of dawn. Soon it will be time to throw myself into the day, to smile and reach out and take care of those around me...soon. But for now, I sit, and breathe, remind myself of so much good in the world, and send energy to friends who need it.

This week with the full moon, my horoscope is all about endings and beginnings. As I look at my life, I realize both are prominent; both are going on right this minute. Transitions are never easy; getting from one place to the next, whether mentally, physically, or emotionally, can sap our energy even when it's a good place to get to. Fighting against the transition, however, does no good and just irritates the pig.[1]

Remember, the Universe has one answer, and that answer is "Yes." If you put out to the Universe that you are *un*worthy of the career, the relationship you crave, the lifestyle you aspire to, the good change to come, the Universe will answer with a resounding YES. Better, then, to put out that you ARE worthy. That you ARE loved. Because again, the Universe will respond with a resounding YES.

It may seem too simple. So be it. Life, I have found, is what we make it. If we make it difficult, it's difficult. If we make it painful, it's gut-wrenching. Let me paraphrase someone (and I don't remember who, my apologies). He who is happy, sees happiness in those around them. He who is angry, sees anger in those around them. I take this to mean we see what we expect to see in those around us.

Perception is everything. And perception can be skewed every-which-way. If you take other people seriously, and your own self maybe not quite so seriously; if you give others your love and trust, and receive that from others in return; if you work on growing your mind and expanding your heart and keeping your body strong, then it is my belief your life will grow in meaning and love.

I look back on my journey since 2010, and even more so since 2013, and I realize how far I've come. I'm a nicer person now. I'm kinder. True, I've had to shore up my shields, because I'm emotionally more available than ever and as an empath, this isn't necessarily good. And yet, I'm a better person, even with more vulnerability. Yeah, I still have a long way to go. But I'm confident I'll get there.

If you don't have nurturing people around you, find them. If you don't have people who believe in you, seek them out. For they are out there.

Believe in others. Nurture others. What goes around comes around, and the more love we can share with the world, the better off we all will be.

It's funny how important it has become to me to spread love in the past three-plus years.

Wherever you go and whatever you do, do it with love and patience in the face of a world that is increasingly demanding your attention, demanding that you to be angry and in a hurry. Defy that demand. Reclaim your peace.

Think seriously about where you put your attention. Is Facebook really worth your time? Instagram? Twitter? These businesses crave your attention. They make money off of your attention. They are not your friends. They are money makers, and you are their cash cow. Maybe it's time to disengage. Maybe it's past time to disengage.

I'm thinking out loud here, after another Tim Ferriss podcast. Please. Educate yourself. Don't be a mindless attention-bot to whatever app happens to have the most investors behind it. Engage your brain. Think for yourself.

Put the cell phone down. Don't respond to the triggers of messages. Truly, life will go on if you don't answer within seconds. You deserve the best of you, and not the leftovers after others' call on your time has ravaged your patience and your creativity.

How would your life look like, if you refused to give your attention away to a bunch of noise?

Take heart in the gentle fall of rain, in the heat of the sun, in the fury of the storm. You are not done yet, there is more to become. Today's burdens are tomorrow's memories, and your attitude is everything.

As Henry Ford said, whether you think you can, or think you can't, you're right. (That was one of my mother's favorite sayings.) So rise. Hold your expectations high, not only for yourself but for those you love. Don't let doubt cripple you; acknowledge it, pat it on the head, and carry on. Don't let disappointment in other people overshadow your own accomplishments. Don't wallow. (Five Minute Rule!)

Know what your goal is and take steps to get there every day. Time waits for no one, and you are the only one who can make your dreams come true.

And if you need the encouragement, take this...I believe in you. So very much.

Sending love. Always.

Christine Ashworth
Simi Valley, California
October 5, 2019

26

READING LIST

I've read, or at least started, all of these books. Enjoy!

Crucial Conversations – Tools for Talking When Stakes Are High by Patterson, Grenny, McMillan, Switzler

Dear Writer, You Need to Quit, by Becca Syme

Deep Work, by Cal Newton

Earth Works: Ceremonies in Tower Time, by H. Byron Ballard

How Emotions are Made, by Lisa Feldman Barrett

Myths to Live By, by Joseph Campbell

New Menopausal Years: Alternative Approaches for Women 30 – 90, by Susun S. Weed

Paganism, an Introduction to Earth-Centered Religions, by Joyce & River Higginbotham

The Bluest Eye, by Toni Morrison

The Journal of Henry David Thoreau, 1837-1861

The Meditations of Marcus Aurelius Antoninus: Illustrated & Unabridged

The Miracle Morning, by Hal Elrod

The Miracle Equation, by Hal Elrod

The Portable Jung, Edited by Joseph Campbell

The Power of Habit, by Charles Duhig

The Rhythm of Success, by Emilio Estefan

The Wisdom of Menopause, by Christiane Northrup, MD

Tribe of Mentors, by Tim Ferriss

Wicca – A Guide for the Solitary Practitioner, by Scott Cunningham

ALL THE FOOTNOTES, RIGHT HERE

2. …and then I turned Fifty

1. I've known Bob since I was seventeen, and just dating Tom Ashworth. Poker games. Roommates. Cheap beer. Good times. He was a groomsman at our wedding in 1980. He has the singing voice of an angel.
2. Thomas W. Ashworth. Check out his IMDB page https://www.imdb.com/name/nm0039329/
3. Tammy Baar is the owner of KidToons in Snowmass, Colorado, a hugely successful children's party company. Tammy is my life-long friend that I consider to be my BFF. We first met while sharing a receptionist job at Live Wires Singing Telegrams in 1981. Our offices were in the Taft Building at the corner of Hollywood and Vine. We were both laid off at the same time in 1983, and … but that's another story.

3. Shift Number Three

1. https://en.wikipedia.org/wiki/Silva_Method
2. https://en.wikipedia.org/wiki/Mindvalley_(company)

4. Podcasts, Books, and Strangers

1. https://getwildfit.com/
2. https://en.wikipedia.org/wiki/Tim_Ferriss
3. https://betterfasteracademy.com/
4. I first met Benebell Wen at the Northwest Tarot Symposium in 2018. She's an amazing person and you should check out her work. https://benebellwen.com/

10. Time Management and Beyond

1. Pema Chodron's book, *Taking the Leap*, discusses the concept of Shenpa. I'm sure other books do, too, but this is where I learned it.
2. Sara Lunsford, Editor of this book, who has all my gratitude and thanks.

25. Winding Down

1. Heinlein quote: "Never try to teach a pig to sing. It wastes your time, and it annoys the pig." I prefer to use 'irritate' instead of 'annoy'.

www.ingramcontent.com/pod-product-compliance
Lightning Source LLC
Chambersburg PA
CBHW031449040426
42444CB00007B/1034